THE LAST PARADISE

THE LAST PARADISE
THE BUILDING OF MARCO ISLAND

Douglas Waitley

The Marco Island Eagle
Marco Island, Florida

Published by The Marco Island Eagle,
Marco Island, Florida, a New York Times Company.

Published 1999. Printed in the United States of America.

Illustration Credits:
pp. 122 (courtesy Neil Bahr)
pp. 29, 104, 125, 136, 146, 147 (courtesy Deltona Corp.)
pp. 9, 49, 58, 62 (courtesy Leonard Llewellyn)
pp. 33 (courtesy Herbert Savage)
pp. 106, 109, 116, 120 (courtesy James Stackpoole)
pp. 8, 31, 38, 45-47, 55-56, 65, 67, 70-71, 75, 77-78, 82, 84, 85, 100-101, 110, 113, 140-141 (courtesy James Vensel)
pp. 149, 151 (courtesy Bruce Wessells)
pp. 152 (courtesy View-finders)

Cover photography by Peter Berec.
Design and layout by Jami Clevenger.

The Last Paradise
The Building of Marco Island

John Thomas Photography

Picture a virtually deserted, swampy island off the south Florida Coast. The year is 1964. Mosquitoes fill the air. The only connection to the mainland is over an ancient swing bridge operated by hand.

Now picture the island six months later. The mosquitoes are under control. There is a handsome beachfront hotel. There are twenty-two model homes. There is a yacht club. An 18 hole championship golf course is laid out and planted. Within two months, 2,500 homesites will have been sold, most of which are on a maze of waterways and canals which eventually will wend almost 100 miles through this tropical paradise.

The account of how Marco Island was built by the Deltona Corporation makes fascinating reading. So, too, does Deltona's later confrontation with the environmentalists, which reached all the way to the Supreme Court.

Much of *The Last Paradise* is taken from first-hand accounts by the persons who actually participated in the making of Marco. The book is illustrated with dozens of never published photos.

DOUGLAS WAITLEY is the author of 13 history-related books, including *Roadside History of Florida*, 1997, Mountain Press; and *The Best Backroads of Florida*, 1999, Pineapple Press.

He is formerly a businessman in Evanston, IL, who now splits his time between Maitland and Marco Island.

Mr. Waitley holds a bachelor of science in business administration and a masters degree in history from Northwestern University.

To Mary, my wife, who found Marco Island in 1972

And to Jeff, my son, who has helped us enjoy many winters there.

Introduction

The *Marco Island Eagle* takes great joy and considerable pride in republishing the out-of- print history book, *The Last Paradise, The Building of Marco Island*, by Douglas Waitley.

Many here and across the nation have described this book as the definitive and most compelling document which traces the history of how modern Marco Island became the community it is.

The book begins with the Mackle brothers' vision of a paradise on Marco, and their efforts to make it so, which ends in defeat, according to Frank Mackle Jr., president of Deltona Corporation. But to those who have read or will read this publication, you have seen or will see the extraordinary imprint the Mackle brothers and their corporation stamped on the shape and social conscience of the island — influencing the direction of the island's future.

But Deltona Corporation was also the beneficiary of earlier pioneers who had similar visions, some born out of necessity, others born of wide-eyed inspiration. You will find them too in this book. But it was Deltona Corporation and its legion of professional employees who created most of the lay of the land that exists today, including Collier Boulevard, Emerald Beach condominiums (the first), all the courts and circles and terraces and all the finger points of land that protrude into the canals and bays, dredged and built from 1964 almost through the 1980s.

It was this remarkable feat that brought thousands to the island to view and to eventually settle. The initial marketing campaign to sell the island to homeowners stretched around the world and was as, or more, ambitious than any other campaign of the time.

On the pages of this book, Mr. Waitley captures in interviews with the chief people responsible for this development the excitement, joy, satisfaction, dedication and ultimately the sadness and disappointment when environmentalists appealed Deltona's plans in court and won.

The dream began to fade. Deltona Corporation was forced to sell off large undeveloped parcels of its holdings. Gone too were the plans for arching some of the islands around Marco to the main island. Eventually as Frank Mackle said, the dream died, it was defeated.

Parts of the book reads like a fast-paced novel, particularly the parts relating to Jim Vensel, who conceived of the design and oversaw the intricate complexity of making the design reality. Or Herbert Savage's search for the right building design for the island, to Neil Bahr's office of marketing which created extraordinary successful satellite real estate offices nationwide.

It has been a pleasure working with Mr. Waitley, who is gracious, sincere and a writer of grace and style. It is an honor for us to publish his work.

We also would like to acknowledge the former publishers' assistance. After a round-the-world search, Stewart and Brenda Beck of the former Pickering Press, which first published the book in 1993, were found and they wished the Eagle all the joy and pleasure with the work as they experienced when they first published it.

Finally, to visitors and residents alike who take for granted the magnificent structure that is named Marco Island, you will find herein what tremendous courage and genius it took to make it reality. We owe Douglas Waitley, the Mackle brothers and Deltona Corporation a deep debt of gratitude.

Ralph Hall
Executive Editor
Marco Island Eagle

Contents

ACKNOWLEDGMENTS

This book would never have been possible without the help and cooperation of Deltona's alumni. Foremost is Frank Mackle, who opened to me the doors of his memories. James Vensel and Neil Bahr gave me innumerable interviews from which I gained considerable insight into Deltona's inner councils. Herbert Savage was a great help, as were Leonard Llewellyn, James Stackpoole, and C. Edward Hinkley. Michelle Garbis, provided me with all of the company's annual reports.

Many other persons not connected with Deltona were of aid. Bernard Yokel, then president of the Florida Audubon Society, gave me several vivid and friendly interviews. Norman Herren provided me with invaluable information about Barron Collier. A. C. Hancock and Wesley Downey gave me their recollections of early politics in Collier County. And many thanks to Barbara Minch, who got me started on this grand adventure.

I am indebted to several persons for the photos, almost all of which have never been published before. Jim Vensel is foremost on my list of donors. I also received excellent photos from Leonard Llewellyn, Neil Bahr, Jim Stackpoole, Herb Savage, and Bruce Wessells. In addition, several pictures and maps were taken from Deltona's annual reports, with the assent of Michelle Garbis. Other maps were used with permission from the Marco Island Rotary Club and the Marco Beach Realty Co. The excellent photo of Marco Shores is courtesy Marco Island's Viewfinders.

To all the above persons, without exception, I say thanks for your help! The book is a tribute to you who played such vital roles in making Marco the wonderful place that it is today.

Prologue

Frank Mackle, once Deltona Company's guiding genius, was old when I met him. His back was bent from a recent fall in the hospital where he had gone after a heart attack and for the angioplasty which followed. He walked with a slow, belabored gait as we moved down the hall toward his office. Pictures of Marco Island lined the walls. Some showed an island overgrown with swampy vegetation. Others pictured Marco when Deltona had just begun converting it into the maze of canals and homesites that was to make it into a paradise – perhaps Florida's last.

When we reached his office, he led me to a fine-grained wooden cabinet where he kept a dozen or so scrapbooks. They were bound with expensive leather jackets and were heavy with memorabilia. We put a few of them on the conference table and opened them at random.

The past leaped out. There he was: a dapper young man in his prime. His brothers, Elliott and Robert, were with him at a horse show. High society. The people bore themselves with the grace of long wealth.

Another page. More memories. Frank's father suave, good looking. Newspaper clippings told about the success of the Mackle Company, which the father had founded many years earlier.

Then the next scrapbook. There was a close-up of the three Mackle brothers. I could see their characters in each face: Elliott, the eldest, a thick neck, broad features, a bull of a man used to quick decisions; Robert, darker, lips pursed, reflective; and Frank, the youngest and most handsome, with an aura of good fellowship and a smile that could turn snow to sunshine. Both his brothers had been dead for many years at the time of the writing of this book in 1994. Frank Mackle died in 1996.

He flipped ahead and I recognized Deltona's headquarters, which was just down Third Avenue from Mackle's current office in 1993. He still received some letters at Deltona even though he resigned in 1985. He had loved that company more than almost anything in life. But he didn't go to the building any more. Instead he sent a messenger once a week to collect his mail.

Our talk turned to Marco Island. Although he was in his mid-70's his voice was firm, his thoughts were clear, and his eyes had fire.

"I couldn't believe Marco the first time I saw it. I had made a special trip over from Miami in '62. We stood on Crescent Beach where the State Road ended and it was fantastic. Just fantastic. I decided right on the spot to turn Marco into a paradise everyone could enjoy. My brothers and I had already developed Key Biscayne, so I knew we could do it!"

He began speaking of his dreams for Marco. "I wanted to develop the island for moderate income persons. The Colliers, who were in partnership with Deltona during the first few years, got angry because we were not building mansions for the wealthy. But I thought middle income people should enjoy the beauties of nature the same as the rich."

At this point Frank Mackle snapped his scrapbook shut and looked me in the eyes.

"I fell in love with that island from the beginning. I had my people plan everything about it with the greatest care. Our homes were oriented towards water views. I insisted on that."

"And the Marco Beach Hotel... have you ever seen such a vista as from our lobby? I'll match it against any in the world! We won many awards for that hotel. It was the finest on the Gulf."

"The hotel made the island. It was my pride. I felt good every time I entered it."

Then he grew silent, deep in reverie. "To have to sell it was a bitter thing." His voice trailed off.

He began to pace his office, though walking was an effort. He was reliving the 1970s when the Army Corps of Engineers denied Deltona the dredge and fill permits necessary to complete development of the island. The denial made it impossible for the company to honor its sales contracts and resulted in a devastating loss to Deltona estimated at more than $100 million. It was a setback from which the company never recovered.

"Many people wanted me to take bankruptcy. That would have wiped out all the debt. Deltona would be prosperous now. But it wasn't the honorable course. I never even contemplated doing such a thing!"

"I was taught in grammar school," Mackle continued, after a moment, "that if you paid good money for a piece of property, you could do whatever you wanted with it... except you couldn't harm your neighbor or do illegal acts. That wasn't so, I found out!"

"One thing people have always said about Florida developers was that they wanted to sell you worthless land underwater. But in my case I wanted to sell a good piece of land that was developed. But they wouldn't let me!"

"I don't know what was in their damned minds! I remember the head of one of those groups, maybe of the Sierra Club, making a speech in which he said there is no such thing as property rights, only environmental rights. Hadn't he heard of the Constitution?"

Frank Mackle was growing tired. "Sorry," he said, "I guess the interview is over. We'll talk more sometime later." He escorted me to the door.

"I tried the best I could," he said in parting. "I gave it a damned good shot. But they beat me."

1

The Dream Begins, 1962

It was a bright morning in 1962. Five men stood on the deserted beach at Marco Island, Florida and gazed in wonderment. They had never seen anything like it. Mile after mile of Florida's whitest sands reached off in a gentle crescent on each side of them. Waves from the Gulf of Mexico murmured softly on the shore, and overhead pelicans and terns wheeled in the sea-misted air.

The beach glistened with thousands of seashells, and on the sand dunes delicate spires of sea oats did pirouettes in the balmy breeze. Back further on the shore leafy mangroves hummed in the wind. The only visible human habitation was a half-dozen low buildings almost lost in the southern distance. This was a missile tracking station built in the late '50s to trace the route of rockets fired from Eglin Air Force Base at Pensacola. It was pretty much out of service now and its personnel usually consisted of a single, lonely attendant.

The men drove along the beach in each direction. What a place! Who wouldn't love to have a residence here: to swim in the Gulf; to stroll the beach collecting shells; to enjoy an evening cocktail on his patio while the sun set in a roiling ocean paint pot.

They stopped the car and talked enthusiastically. A luxury hotel could go here and up the beach would be high-rise condos. There would be a public bathing beach in between.

On the northern end was an inlet to a calm-water bay: boating docks and channels could be put there.

They had been told there was no undeveloped location in southern Florida like Marco Island, and they were beginning to believe it.

Enter the Mackle Brothers

The five men were the top officials of the Deltona Corporation. Jim Vensel was a brilliant architect and city planner; and Neil Bahr was an ace sales executive. But the guiding geniuses were the three Mackle brothers. Elliott was the oldest. He had an uncanny ability to pick out good land for development. He was considered somewhat opinionated and sometimes made snap decisions. He was counterbalanced by Robert, tallest of the three. Robert ran the day-to-day construction operations. It was he who dealt with the unions and saw to it that relations remained smooth. He was a snappy dresser and loved golf as nothing else.

Frank Mackle, the youngest of the three, was the coordinator. He was a master at public relations and corporate affairs. He was soft-spoken, but forceful. And he had a winning smile that reflected his sincerity and basic honesty. Congenial, handsome, good-natured, Frank was the leader and Deltona's president. Yet company decisions were made by the three brothers unanimously. They thought as one and even shared the same office.

The Mackles, Bahr, and Vensel had made the three-hour drive from their home office in Miami because they had been approached by representatives of the Collier Corp., who owned most of Marco Island and were looking for a responsible developer to turn it into the tropical paradise old Barron Collier had dreamed of when he purchased it in 1922. Recently his son, Barron Jr., had read a complimentary article about the Mackles in *Business Week* and had made a personal trip to see them. "He came to my office," Frank Mackle recalled, "and asked me if I'd ever been to Marco Island. He told me he thought we'd be the perfect company to develop it....I drove over there, and I couldn't believe what I saw."

The Missile Tracking Station

The Mackles, with Vensel and Bahr, made a thorough inspection of the island that day. First they headed to the missile tracking station. The base road, which connected with State Route 92 (S.R. 92) a few hundred yards from the beach, was broad and made of concrete. The first segment ran straight as a rocket for 6,000 feet. It was obvious that with the addition of an apron on each side it could easily be converted to a landing strip for small planes.

They met the watchman. He gladly showed them around, happy to have visitors. He kept the station ready for action, with air conditioners maintaining a cool temperature for the banks of computers in the spacious communications building. The Air Force had not used the facility since Fidel Castro had complained about the missiles from Pensacola. It was only a matter of time until it would close the site and the half-dozen buildings be available for other uses.

Except for the Air Force's short access road, Marco had only two real thoroughfares. S.R. 92 started at the Tamiami Trail (U.S. 41) and entered the island on an ancient wooden swing bridge installed in 1938 after being barged down from its original site in Fort Myers. On the island, the road continued to the beach. Midway through Marco, it

A Portion of the Missile Tracking Station, 1964.

The Air Force used this base on Cape Marco for a short time in the late 1950s to track missiles dispatched from Eglin Air Force Base near Pensacola. The Air Force had leased the site from Barron Collier's company and returned it when the base was no longer needed.

By then the Colliers had formed the Marco Island Development Corp.(MIDC) with Deltona. MIDC took over the Air Force buildings and used them as its construction headquarters.

This photo was taken in 1964. Crescent Beach stretches far into the distance without any sign of habitation.

The site is now occupied by luxury condominium high rises.

crossed the other road, S.R. 953. It was the island's original pathway. It dated back to the days when there were two tiny settlements: the village of Marco on the northern tip and Caxambas on the southern.

As the Deltona executives drove back east on S.R. 92, they crossed a narrow belt of mangroves and wetlands that fringed the beach and quickly reached S.R. 953. The land was dry here and spotted with sand pines, saw palmetto, and some live oaks. Five hundred years ago this had been the shoreline.

Marco around 1962.

This view of Marco presents the island much the way the Mackles must have found it when they made their initial trip in 1962. S.R. 92 crosses the photo from left to right and S.R. 953 from top to bottom. Collier Boulevard does not exist at this time. When Deltona builds it in 1964, it will cross between Collier Bay at the upper left and Smokehouse Bay beneath it.

We are looking north with the Gulf of Mexico at the top left and the Marco River reaching across the upper portion of the picture. The cleared land across the river is the Isles of Capri development. The village of Marco faces the Isles. The old sand road to Marco can be seen to the upper left of S.R. 953. The early settler's cemetery still exists near the junction.

The development in the photo's center is the Highlands, dating back to the 1890s.

The clearing for the railroad turnaround is on the far right. The elementary school is just below the turnaround.

Roadway of failures

This crossroads was to have been the center of Collier City when Barron Collier, advertising magnate from New York City, began selling lots back in 1927. As they headed north on S.R. 953, they passed on their right the burned-out ruins of Collier's old power plant. It had never been used, for the Depression had put an end to his plans.

A mile down the road they came to another defunct real estate venture called the Marco Highlands. This dated back many years and consisted of a few streets unimaginatively named First Avenue, Second Avenue, and so on. A mile and a half farther north was the hamlet of Marco, located on the Marco River, where S.R. 953 ended. Once there had been a ferry at this point connecting the village with the mainland, but the installation of the bridge on S.R. 92 had put it out of business.

Captain Bill Collier: Heroics and Heartbreak

The village of Marco had been founded shortly after the Civil War by a Tennessean, W. T. Collier, who was no relation to Barron. W. T. and his wife, Barbara. He built a home from lumber they carried with them to the island. Three months after completion, the house burned down – thus starting the sequence of hard luck that was to play such a prominent part in Marco's early history.

The Colliers and their children had lived in a palmetto shack for several years. During this time they began farming cabbages, which they exported to Key West. Gradually a few more families moved to this torrid, bug-infested island, and in the 1880s when a sailing vessel began making regular trips to the market at Key West, Collier opened a store.

Soon one of W. T.'s sons, William D., better known as Captain Bill, was named postmaster of Malco, as Marco was called in the postal files, because some higher up thought, mistakenly, there was another Marco in the state. In 1888 Captain Bill suffered a tragedy. Having opened a boat yard in Marco, he took one of his vessels on a trip to Key West. Just 18 miles from his destination, he encountered a violent squall. The boat overturned and nine persons drowned. Among them were three of the captain's young sons.

Captain Bill did not let the tragedy stop him. When fishermen, hearing about Marco's bountiful catches, began to frequent the island, he turned his home into a hotel with 20 sleeping rooms and a dining room. It was a splendid structure for such a remote island. For bathers he even hacked out a sand and shell road over to the Gulf beaches a mile southwest.

Barron Collier, buying up the island in 1922, supposedly approached Captain Bill with the purpose of obtaining the village of Marco, too. Apparently the Captain asked a price that Barron felt was too high, for the deal was never consummated and the little cluster of buildings at the northern tip of the island (as well as the Highlands in the island's center) remained out of the corporate holdings.

The Marco Inn continued to be a popular destination not only for fishermen, but for people from Naples, who boated to it for fine seafood dinners. A ferocious hurricane in 1960 removed it from its foundation, yet the inn was still active when the Deltona group stopped for lunch three years later.

The Deltona executives, in their dress shirts and neckties, were conspicuous among the salty fishermen. Nevertheless they let everyone speculate as to their purpose, for the operation at this stage was quite hush. Vensel, gazing around the interior, was impressed with the walls, which were covered by hundreds of tarpon scales. When one was caught, a scale was removed, monogrammed to save the fisherman's name for posterity, and nailed to the wall.

After a brief interlude at the Inn, the visitors were on their way once more. They went back south along S.R. 953, passing a small trailer park on the Marco River close to the Inn. Next to the trailer camp were ruins of the old Doxsee clam factory. It was a sorry sight now, for just the walls and some rusting machinery remained. Yet from its founding in

1911 until its demise in 1947, when the clam beds were depleted, the factory had been one of the mainstays of Marco.

The Death of a Railroad

The Doxsee factory, as well as a second clam cannery at the Caxambas end of the island, was a basic reason for the construction of a railroad to Marco in 1927. Barron Collier regarded the railroad of such importance that he planned Collier City close to its terminus.

But the railroad did not take on the importance that Collier hoped. It never had a station, just a turnaround and a loading platform on some low dunes. Diminishing clam shipments brought its abandonment in the mid-1940s.

The rail bed made a decent trail for the Deltona men, who guided their auto onto it and drove across the northeastern portion of the island to the point where the tracks had ascended an embankment that connected with a bridge over the Marco River. The bridge was gone, so they stopped their car on the embankment and got out to look over the river, an ideal site for another bridge sometime in the future.

It was at this point that they encountered one of the island's perils. "We were instantly covered with mosquitoes," Vensel recalled. "We didn't dare swat them for we were in our white shirts and would have had blood all over. We ran back to our car. It was the worst I've ever seen!"

Then the executives continued down route S.R. 953, past S.R. 92, into the southern part of Marco. The area they passed through had once been a pineapple plantation owned by Frederick Ludlow. Now the plantation was gone and the land had reverted to its natural vegetation.

The Calusa Tribe: Shells and Sharks

In the days of the Calusa Indians the south had been a separate island. Remains of the Calusa were everywhere. There was a nationally famous excavation site near the Marco Inn, where Captain Bill had discovered what turned out to be one of the richest treasures of Indian artifacts unearthed anywhere in Florida. A lovely wooden carving subsequently called the Key Marco Cat, in particular, became a prize possession of the Smithsonian Institution. The Calusa were a hardy, seafaring tribe. They apparently relished the dangerous occupation of hunting down sharks, whose teeth were highly valued for weapons and saws.

That the Calusa lived mainly on clams was apparent as the Deltona group drove the road which hugged the neck of land with Barfield Bay to the right and Indian Hill on the left. Indian Hill, which was the highest point on the island, consisted of a long clamshell mound fifty-one feet high topped with cactus. It may have started as an Indian garbage dump, but later it probably developed into a ceremonial site. Whatever the case, the founding family of Caxambas, James and Tommie Barfield, found it an ideal site upon which to construct their home.

The Barfields and Old Caxambas

The Barfields grew pineapples along the road and opened a general store on the wharf in the vicinity where Tony Roberts, Caxambas' first settler, lived several decades earlier. All that remained of Roberts in 1908 was his name on the bay. Soon the Barfields turned their home into a hotel, which they appropriately called The Heights.

Prosperity peaked in the tiny community after the Burnham clam factory was erected on the waterfront near the site of the artesian well, called Caxambas by the Caribbean Indians, where Spanish ships once replenished their water casks. But the factory closed in 1929 and the village never recovered.

By the time that the Deltona party was scouting the area, all that remained of Caxambas was the decaying clam plant and a small cluster of ramshackle wooden shacks called the Ideal Fish Camp. There were not even any homes. For when Collier had purchased the island, he had also obtained automatic ownership of the buildings. Then in 1949, his descendants, deciding to develop the island, moved all the homes to the village of Goodland, just south of the S.R. 92 bridge to the mainland. Nothing came of all this effort, however.

The Deltona executives climbed Indian Hill to gain a view of the island. The Heights Hotel was gone, having been moved with the rest of Caxambas, and only the crumbling foundation remained. Barron Collier had planned to make Caxambas into an important seaport. But that was past history. What they wanted to see was the island. And the panorama was magnificent!

To the south, the Ten Thousand Island beaches churned the Gulf waters into liquid pearls. Here the verdure of limitless mangrove trees melded with the turquoise of tropical water and the saffron ringlets of virgin sands. To the north, Marco itself reached out like a vast Persian carpet done in greens and blues and olives. And to the west. Ah, to the west. There was that luscious beach that had lured them to the island in the first place. The lowering sun was flinging diamonds onto the waves. There was a marvelous sunset in the making.

Having now traveled the $5\frac{1}{2}$ miles from Marco's tip to toe, the men turned back toward Miami. They crossed over to the mainland on the crude swing bridge which the keeper turned to close like one would

The state of Florida.

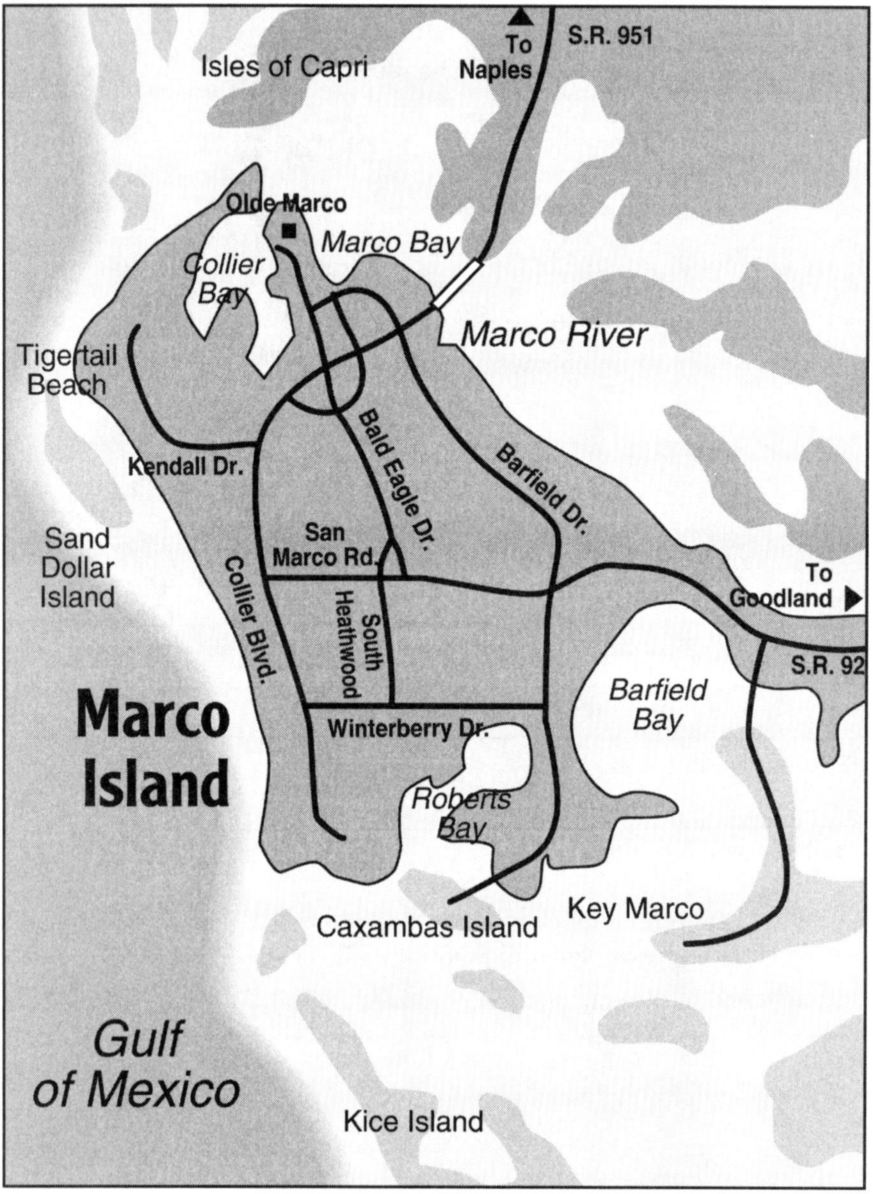

The Marco Island area today.

unscrew a tin of sardines. Then they passed through almost endless stands of mangroves, their roots grasping the watery muck beneath with gracefully grotesque fingers.

Marco's Challenge

Despite Marco's beauty there were many negatives to development of the island. The mosquitoes were one, for they must be controlled – but how? ...and at what cost? Then, too, the island must have sewer facilities. Also there must be a dependable water source to replace the current dependency on gathered rain water.

Another disadvantage was that the location was so remote from civilization. Would this cause prospective buyers to reject homes or lots here for lack of cultural and recreational facilities? Even Naples, 12 miles north, was not much more than a hick town; and the entire Collier County had less than 16,000 persons. Then, too, would Northerners want to purchase in a locale that had no major airport?

Could they find a bank that would loan them money for such a daring venture? And even if they got their initial construction loan, what if the sales did not go as fast as projected and they needed more money. That's where a major financial crunch might catch them!

The whole island was a graveyard of other persons' hopes and dreams. Ruins were almost everywhere. Weren't the warnings vivid enough?

To add to their concerns was the fact that they had never done anything like this before. It wasn't Marco's size, which initially was 10,327 acres, including 6,700 on Marco itself and the rest on the adjacent mainland. They had completed developments far larger. Indeed, Port Charlotte, which the Mackles had begun back in 1956 (when they ran another company known as General Development), reached up to 118,000 acres and spanned three Florida counties for 185 square miles! But the work at Port Charlotte consisted primarily of laying out roads and selling lots.

Their actual construction experience was mainly with retirement communities, like the town of Deltona, just north of Orlando, which was their current project. It was on 15,000 acres of rolling land and all they had to do was drape the streets along the hills and put in the homes.

With Marco it would be entirely different. Now they were talking about building a resort community literally from the ground up. The construction of homes would be almost incidental! This was to be a vacation paradise, with boating, swimming, fishing, and golf. With this in mind, swamplands must be converted into clean-water bays lined with boat slips and homes. Thus, there would be dredging and land filling and the construction of seawalls and bridges. In addition, there must be a marina for boaters and an 18-hole golf course for golfers.

Deltona would have to form the island's utility company and put in sewer and water lines. Furthermore precise city planning must be done, with areas allotted for schools and churches as well as for residences. There must be several commercial zones; and the stores must be leased and ready to operate when people began moving in. Streets had to be paved and streetlights put in. An airplane landing field must be constructed. And provision must be made for visitors at a hotel that must be run with pride and efficiency.

Such an undertaking had seldom been done in Florida. It would be a challenge that would fall primarily on the shoulders of the five men in the car.

"We thought long and hard about taking on Marco," Neil Bahr confided. "The decision to go ahead was major. We had done nothing like it before. But there was that gorgeous sugar beach! I knew we could do it."

The Fateful Decision

In the end it was an emotional choice. The island had an enchantment that captured the imagination of the hardened businessmen. "Marco Island's topography and tropical foliage give it a character unmatched in this part of the world," Frank Mackle would tell his stockholders. Although Mackle promised them nice profits from the operation there was more to it than that. He earnestly wanted to construct a place of which he could be proud. "The company is determined that the community it builds at Marco Island will be in keeping with the island's natural beauty, he promised.

So the decision was made even while they sped back through the Everglades. They would tackle the complicated Marco project if they could reach an agreement with the Colliers.

As soon as he reached his office in Miami, Frank Mackle phoned the Colliers. He was ready to start serious negotiations.

The saga of triumph and crushing defeat was about to commence.

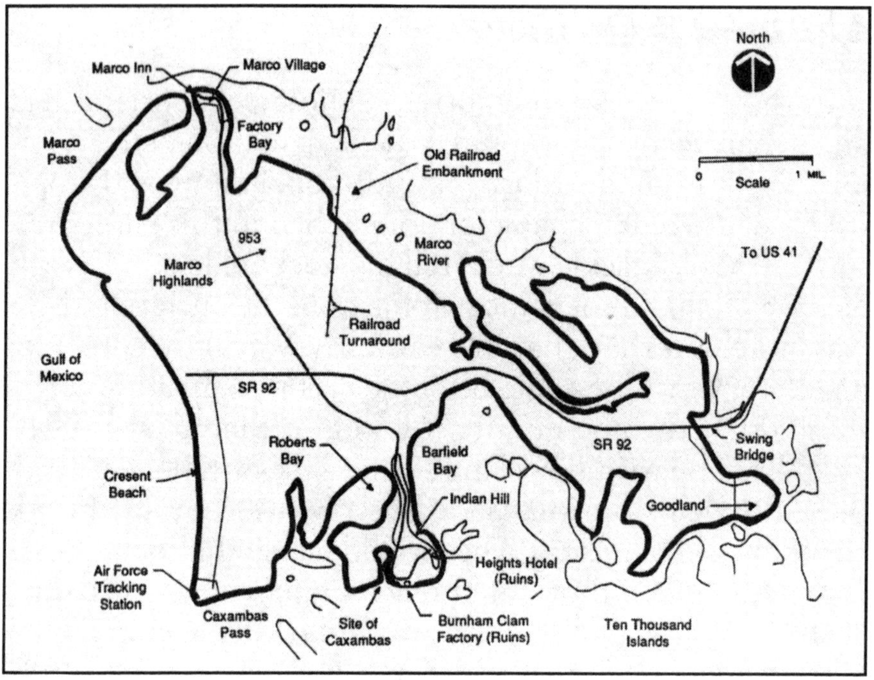

Marco Island in 1962.

2

PREPARATIONS, 1963-64

Although the Deltona executives were enthusiastic about Marco Island, there remained many knotty problems. The first was to hammer out a workable agreement with the Colliers.

The Sad Tale of Barron Collier and His Three Sons

The years had not dealt kindly with Barron Collier Sr. He once had dreams of developing Marco, but the Great Depression had devastated Barron's advertising empire and put his plans on hold.

Barron Sr., died quite suddenly of a stroke in 1939. He left his vast estate of 900,000 acres, 12 Florida hotels, and a phone company to his three sons, Barron Jr., Sam, and Miles. The federal government claimed a goodly share of Barron's assets in the form of estate taxes. But his land and buildings were not easily salable on short notice, so the Colliers and their lawyers worked out a 10-year plan with the IRS whereby a certain portion of the assets would be sold at favorable times over that period to meet the taxes.

The tax matter was finally settled by 1949, and it was at this time that the Collier sons made plans to develop Marco. They moved the homes at the Caxambas (southern) end to Goodland, still on the island, but off their property. However, at this moment tragedy struck. Young Sam was killed in a racing incident at Watkins Glen, N.Y. This meant once again more estate taxes and further reorganization. The two remaining brothers, Barron Jr., and Miles, bought out Sam's heirs and within a few years were ready to act again on their Florida holdings. But at this moment Miles, the youngest of the brothers, went in the hospital with a respiratory virus. Within 12 hours he had died of a rare form of polio! Both brothers were gone before their 40th birthdays.

This seemed to take the drive from Barron Jr., a quiet, introverted man. Although Barron sold his house in New York and bought residences in Naples and Palm Beach, he did not have the spirit, nor the stamina, for the large scale development that Marco would have required. Indeed, after a serious lung operation, doctors advised the tall, genteel man not to participate in business on a day-to-day basis. Thereafter he had to content himself with periodic visits to the Naples headquarters.

Managing the Collier's business was Norman Herren, a native Floridian and graduate of the University of Miami. Herren had been with the Colliers from the days of Barron Sr., and knew the operations down to the smallest tin shed. Although the family was splitting into two factions, one oriented toward Barron Jr., and the other toward the descendants of Miles, Herren was able to keep them both together and prevent the split-up that was still a decade and a half in the future.

Herren had been a key man in the plans to develop the Collier property and it had been most frustrating. "Each time we started, something tragic happened," he lamented to me. With the deaths, illnesses, and family controversies, it was obvious that the Colliers were in no shape to deal with Marco.

So it was that Herren began looking for someone interested in the island.

One of the most appealing ideas was to sell Marco to the State of Florida for a nature preserve. Conservationist Bernard Yokel heard that the Colliers offered the island for $1 million. It would have been a tremendously advantageous purchase for the state. But the proposal was refused!

Marco and the Aluminum Plant

With the State not interested, the Colliers turned to others. "We listened to a lot of different ideas," Herren said, "but nothing ever seemed to happen."

Finally interest was shown by an investor from Colorado. He wanted to make Marco and neighboring Kice Islands into a major facility for the importation of bauxite from Jamaica and oil from Venezuela. Deep-water dredging would enable large ships to make port. Kice Island would have an aluminum smelter and oil refinery. Marco would be built up with workers' homes.

Plans were drawn in secret. "There was no publicity about it," former Collier County Commissioner, Wesley Downey, confided. "But I saw the drawings. They were in color. Harmon Turner, our county manager, had them in his office. Very few people knew about them. It was shocking to me. It would have changed everything!"

Herren confirmed the investor's plan. "He did go into details with us. But it never went beyond conversation."

The Colliers Seek Out the Mackles

Although the Collier people would listen to any offer, they were actively pursuing the Mackles – particularly after

Barron Jr.'s, visit to Deltona's Miami headquarters early in 1962. Even as the Colorado industrialist was readying his plans, Herren continued follow-up overtures with the Mackles. He had Jeff Hudson, from Stone and Webster Service Corp., the Collier's management company, send a letter to the Mackles. Dispatched May 24, 1962, Hudson's letter was the first written communication between the Colliers and the Mackles and may be taken as the conception date for the island's development.

Hudson enclosed two maps, one of Marco with the Collier's holdings delineated, and another showing the sources of potable water on the mainland (there were none that he knew of on the island itself). It had been on the basis of these maps that the Mackles, Vensel, and Bahr would make their initial inspection tour of Marco.

The Tricky Negotiations to Buy Marco

Negotiations between Deltona and the Collier people went along smoothly. Because development of the swampy island was primarily an engineering problem, Herren dealt mainly with Elliott Mackle, who had a degree in engineering from Washington and Lee University. Elliott, age 52, was the eldest of the Mackle brothers. He had joined the family owned business back in 1930, when it was run by Frank Sr., the company's English-born founder. After the death of his father 11 years later, Elliott had headed the company. During World War II, while Robert and Frank were in the service, it was Elliott who had directed the construction of the gigantic Naval base at Key West, for which the Mackle company had won the coveted Army/Navy E, awarded only to those firms displaying excellence in military work.

Herren had been impressed with the Mackles for many years. He knew that they had done a beautiful job converting Key Biscayne, at Miami's front door, into a showplace that attracted such celebrities as Richard Nixon. He also knew that, after the Mackles had teamed up with the General Development Corp. (GDC) in 1954, they had built more than 5,000 homes and created 100,000 homesites in Port Charlotte, Port Saint Lucie, Port Malabar, Sebastian and Vero Beach Highlands, Pompano Beach Highlands and in other GDC communities. Indeed, with the Mackle brothers running GDC, it became the nation's top homebuilder in 1958 and for several years thereafter.

But 1961, as the result of a bitter management squabble, the Mackles sold their General Development interests and soon formed a new company, which promptly purchased 15,000 choice homesite acres near Deland and Daytona Beach. The development was called "Deltona" after its location, and the new company also adopted this name.

Because the Mackles had demonstrated such success with Florida real estate, Herren shared with Barron Collier Jr., the confidence that a joint venture with them was the way to bring Marco to its proper fulfillment. "The Mackles had the planners, the engineers, the equipment, and the marketing organization," Herren told me. "They were probably the foremost developers in Florida, if not the nation. Their reputation was impeccable. We felt comfortable with them."

A Rare Thing: A Contract Based on Trust

The agreement that finally emerged could only have been consummated in an atmosphere of trust – particularly on the Colliers' part. For openers, the agreement created the Marco Island Development Corp. (MIDC), owned

50 percent by the Colliers and 50 percent by Deltona. Although both parties put up $750,000 as equity capital in return for MIDC stock, the Colliers gave MIDC a loan of $2.25 million, whereas Deltona loaned only $750,000. Thus Deltona furnished only a third of the capital but gained half ownership.

Furthermore, Deltona obtained its $1.5 million contribution from a bank loan which used Marco Island itself as collateral. By this means Deltona bought into the deal using none of its own money!

As far as the actual purchase of the island, the price was established at $7 million, far in excess of that for which the state had considered paying several years earlier. However, the Colliers would not start receiving the money until 1968, and then over a period of six years. The payment plan extended over such a long period in order for Deltona to obtain the funds needed through sales. Thus Deltona would not have to spend any of its own money in order to obtain the island. Meanwhile the Colliers would receive no interest on the sum outstanding.

On the surface it seemed as if the Colliers were not only giving their island away, but paying for the privilege. Yet when questioned about the arrangement, Norm Herren expressed complete satisfaction with it. After all, it had been negotiated for the Colliers by a top New York lawyer, who was well aware of the dangers. But he accepted the Mackles on their sterling reputation. "Besides," Herren said, "Deltona did not get in free. The company contributed the experts and did all the developmental work. We realized we would have to put in considerable capital in addition to the land and that there would be no immediate return. That's how it is when you begin from scratch. It was a very, very large project. We knew we would have to be patient until it turned a profit in later years. We trusted the men in charge of Deltona."

Although Barron Collier was chairman and other Collier people occupied half the seats on the eight-man MIDC Board of Directors, it was Frank, Elliott, and Robert, as president, vice president, and secretary-treasurer. Once construction began, the MIDC treasurer, Robert Mackle, would begin writing checks to Deltona treasurer, Robert Mackle, for the cost of construction plus a profit for Deltona of 5percent. And, when the land sales started, more checks would flow from Mackle to Mackle as Deltona received its profit of 3 percent on the land which had been sold.

The agreement provided obvious conflicts of interest concerning the Mackles. I asked Herren if he had experienced any questionable dealings under this arrangement. "No," he said. "The Mackles never betrayed the trust that was the essence of the contract."

The arrangement continued amicably until 1968 when Deltona acquired the Collier interest in exchange for 136,250 shares of Deltona's stock. Since the stock was then selling for $55 per share, this represented $7,500,000, the full price for the island plus a little extra. Again, Deltona had done it with no transfer of cash!

"A New and Different Sort of Planned Community"

Negotiations between the Colliers and the Mackles extended over a considerable period, for this was a major undertaking with a multitude of ramifications. But even while the talks continued, Deltona moved ahead on other fronts.

There were many meetings held in the large office occupied by the Mackle brothers at their new three-story headquarters at 3250 S.W. Third Avenue, Miami. Vensel, Bahr, and a few of the other top executives would talk with Frank, Elliott, and Robert Mackle almost every morning. They would sit around the coffee table and discuss the events not only relating to Marco but what was happening at their recent other purchases in Tampa, Orlando, Daytona Beach, Maitland and, most of all, at the town of Deltona, which was actually their principal development at this time.

The relationships at the company were easy-going and informal. "We were like a family," Vensel recalled. Bahr, in charge of sales, found it an exhilarating experience: "In the early days I loved to go to work. I was routinely in my office at 6:30. And I wasn't the only one there. We felt good about what we were doing! Things were going on!"

One of the things that excited the Deltona people was that, at Marco, they were about to embark on a course that had rarely been taken in development circles. Early on it was decided that Marco, due partly to its rather isolated location, must be "a new and different sort of planned community," in the words of Frank Mackle.

It would not be enough to do a minimum amount of improvement at Marco, then sell the nearly raw lots for an overpriced figure, as the nearby 113,000-acre Golden Gate Estates project, just east of Naples, was doing. On the contrary, Deltona wished to present buyers with a quality, finished job at Marco. And that would mean running fresh water to the property and providing sewage facilities. It would mean building a shopping center and putting up and staffing a hotel for visitors and guests. It would mean providing locations for churches and public beaches and landscaped parks. "Our real objective," Frank Mackle proudly told his stockholders, "is the construction of full communities." The company would be there for the long haul. And that put Deltona on a vastly higher plane than the average build-and-run developer all too common in Florida at the time.

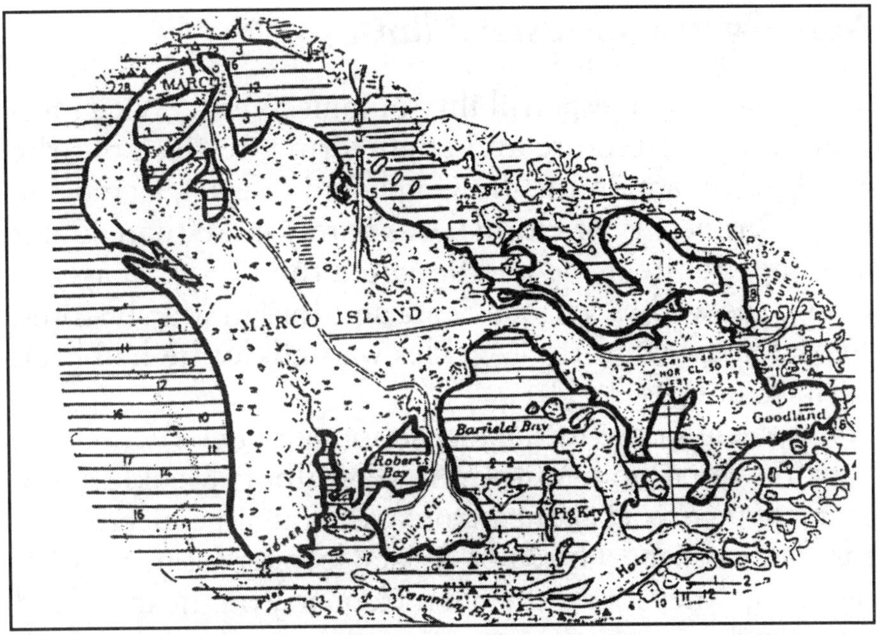

Marco Island in the late 1920s as it appeared on a government survey.

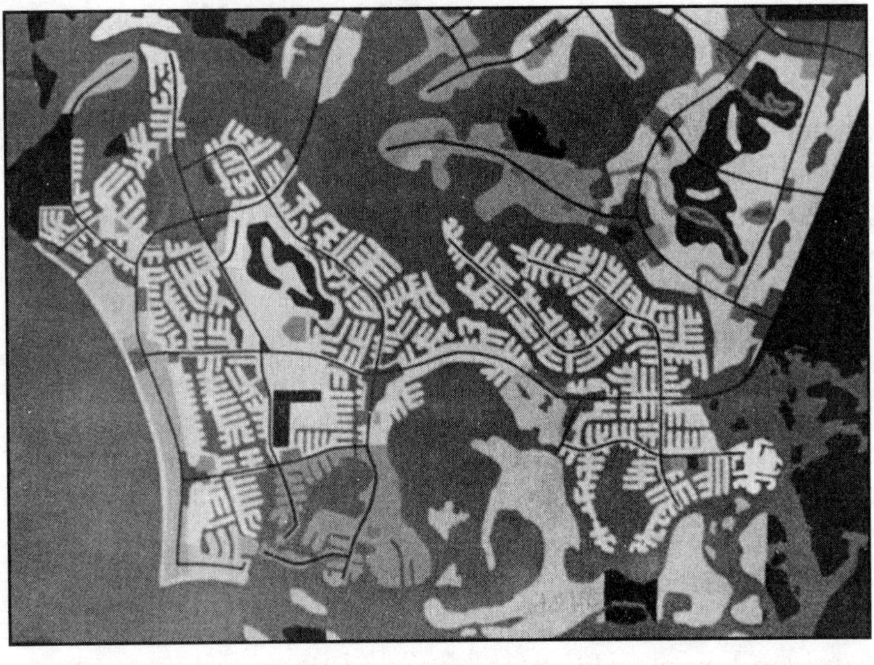

Marco according to Deltona's 1964 plan. The right half of the sketch was never developed because the company was refused a dredge and fill permit by the federal government in 1976.

Marco gets its Master Plan

It became the responsibility of James Vensel, vice president for architecture and engineering, to flesh out the Mackles' dream on the drawing board. Vensel, a graduate of the University of Florida, was barely more than 30. As a young architect, he had designed the U.S. Embassy in Congo, as well as various Sears and Jordan Marsh stores. Vensel knew what the Mackles wanted, for he had been with them since 1954.

A week after the initial inspection of Marco, Vensel was back on the island. With him were Elliott Mackle and a group of technical people. One of their main concerns was to locate a dependable source of potable water. Using the Colliers' map, they found the old rock quarry on the mainland seven miles north of Marco. It was brimming with fresh water and was owned by the Colliers. Of course, using it would mean installing a pumping station there and running a water main under the Tamiami Trail (U.S. 41) as well as beneath the Marco River, and constructing a purification plant on the island itself. It could be done, but it would be expensive.

So they tried to find a water source on the island itself. Vensel brought in a digging rig on the back of a truck. He went down 30 feet. Although he located some water there, it was not enough to pursue.

Over the next few months Vensel and his experts returned to Marco many times. They quickly saw that the Colliers' map was incorrect. Drawn from a 1886 survey, it had omitted a half-mile in the center of the island. The Colliers agreed to have a new survey done. By February 1963 the aerial photos were complete. Then surveyor Carl Johnson and his four crews walked over nearly every foot of shell, sand, and muck taking readings and setting their concrete markers.

Original plat drawing of Marco Island.

This is a portion of the original street and lot plats of Marco Island drawn by Deltona architect James Vensel over Memorial Day weekend, 1964. The underlying map is a survey based on aerial photos taken the prior year. The street arching across the upper left portion of the photo is Collier Boulevard. It ends at the Marco River, the large, dark body of water across the upper right. Here it awaits the bridge that will be constructed several years later. Barfield Drive crosses Collier in the middle left. The site of the Yacht Club is lettered in faintly just above Collier at the river The first waterway homes will soon be built on Chestnut Court, the third projection to the left of the Yacht Club.

The golf course has already been drawn at the lower left. The thin finger of land projecting into the Marco River at the upper right is the old railroad bridge embankment.

When the survey was completed, it was given to Vensel. And on Memorial Day weekend, 1964, he sat down with the survey sheets to draw in the streets, the canals, and the individual lots.

Present at the Creation

A virtual blank space lay before Vensel as he laid out the series of 16-by-11 inch survey sheets. S.R. 92 crossed the photos from east to west, and S.R. 953 from north to south. The Gulf of Mexico and the Marco River were black areas, for the photos were negatives. The mangroves and other vegetation were gray splotches. Swampy areas, creeks, and shallow bays were darker gray. Johnson's thin, white elevation lines squiggled across the surface.

From here imagination took over. "I worked alone in the deserted office for four days," Vensel recalled. "The holiday meant nothing to me. I was there each day and far into the night. My wife understood that I was doing something big. We had four little kids, but they didn't see much of me that holiday."

One of the main features Vensel took into account were the swampy areas. Part of them would be dredged and deepened to form lagoons. The dredged material would be deposited around the edges to form dry land.

Thus, far from being obstructions, the swamps were highly valuable, both as waterways and sources of fill material. Although much of the swampy areas were thick with mangroves, the trees were easy to topple and could help form the projections of land that would support Vensel's streets and homesites.

As for the streets, S.R. 92 would stay as it was, ending at the beach, just south of which Vensel drew a wide lot for the hotel that would serve the hordes of visitors who

Herbert Savage and James Vensel at the Marco Beach Hotel around 1967.

Vensel is on the right. It was he, as head of Deltona's Architecture and Engineering Department, who laid out Marco as we know it today. He named the streets and allotted the land for the residences, businesses, hotels, churches, and condominiums. Savage was Vensel's chief assistant. He was responsible for designing most of Deltona's major buildings on Marco. This included the Voyager Hotel, then called the Marco Beach. A few years later he would design the big hotel, now owned by Marriott. Their wives relax with them at poolside. Marie Vensel is in the light sweater and Emily Savage in the dark dress.

would soon be flocking to the now largely deserted island. S.R. 953 would no longer go through to old Caxambas, for a widened Roberts Bay would block its route.

Vensel routed a new throughway to the Caxambas area. This he named Barfield Drive, after the pioneer family who had once owned the Heights Hotel. Vensel also ran a major road along the Gulf beachfront, which he called Collier Boulevard. Was it named in honor of Captain Bill or Barron? "Take your pick," Vensel told me. In any event, it is clear for whom Vensel named Elkcam Circle, the key roadway that he designed around the new commercial center of Marco. Elkcam spelled "Mackle" backwards. It was a trademark of Deltona and appeared in all the company's developments. Vensel thought about sneaking in a byway for himself, but decided Lesnev Lane (Vensel backwards) was too awkward.

Later on Vensel would get around to naming the rest of the nearly 400 byways. The Indians received recognition with Calusa Court. And their place name for the southern part of the island, "Caxambas," became both a Drive and a Court. Some of the pioneers would also be remembered. There was Doxee Terrace (after the early clam factory owners, the Doxsee family – which Vensel told me he just plain misspelled). Pettit Court (after the founder of Goodland, where the old swing bridge crossed to the mainland), and Ludlow Road (after one of the first large-scale farmers). Vensel got their names from books on Marco. Kirk Terrace was named after Bud Kirk, long time charter fisherman and later marine consultant with Deltona.

The matter of coming up with hundreds of street names was something Vensel had encountered before. He had been involved with large developments when he was with General Development, as well as more recently at the town of Deltona. It seemed as if he was always searching for good names. "It got so that almost every time I traveled I'd bring back a street map and have our secretary check them out against the names we kept in a pair of foot-long card files. If it was not in there, she'd make out a new card and insert it. There were a lot of names from Columbus, Ohio in our files, as well as some from New York, Atlanta, Phoenix, and San Francisco."

In locating the commercial heart at the far northern end of the island rather than at the more logical crossroads of the county and state highways, Vensel was assuming that the isolated site would become central when the state, hopefully, approved a bridge across the Marco River near the site of the destroyed railroad span.

When he was through, Vensel had provided for 10,839 homesites along with other areas for apartments, condominiums, hotels and motels. He had artfully arranged a maze of 91 miles of canals so that three-fourths of the lots would be on a waterfront. He had managed to squeeze in a golf course and a yacht club and still allow 275 acres for business and commercial facilities. In addition, he had provided sites for five schools and 17 churches.

It was a masterpiece that was accepted by the Mackles almost as it was roughed out over that Memorial Day weekend in 1964. Of course, there was ultimately a formal presentation. But long before that Vensel had shown general sketches to the Mackles and other Deltona executives. Their reaction was, in Vensel's words, usually: "Oh good. Hurry up!"

That was the way it was. "Marco was special," Vensel recalled. "Everyone was eager to get it going."

3

The Construction Starts, 1964-65

Deltona was more than ready to spring into action when in early June 1964, the agreement with the Colliers was signed.

The date for the Grand Opening of the island was now set for January 31 of the following year. It would be at the height of the tourist season. Not only would prospective buyers be eager to visit the site, but the weather would be at its subtropical finest. Furthermore, the mosquitoes would be in abeyance. Thus it was crucial to have the island in shape by that time. Much later and the season would be lost.

Six Months to Create a Slice of Paradise

The half-year until the Grand Opening gave Deltona precious little time. First, there were the permits to obtain: the zoning and bulkhead go-aheads from the county, the installment OK from the state, and approval from both the state and federal governments for the dredge and fill operation that was the essence of Vensel's intricate canal system.

And this was only the beginning. There was the matter of drinking water. This involved constructing a pumping station at the rock quarry lake 9 miles from Marco, then running a waterline through the swamp bordering the island and under the wide Marco River to a purification

Looking west from the Marco River, October 1964.

The abandoned railroad embankment projects into the river at the bottom. Smokehouse Bay can be seen at the upper part of the photo, with Collier Bay to its right. Collier Boulevard has not been built yet.

The canals in the right front area have been dug but the seawall slabs have not been placed. The dike separating the canals from the river is still in place and the water appears to have been pumped down to a level where the slabs can be installed The Yacht Club will be built on the piece of land fronting the river. At about the same time, pavement will be laid for Buttonwood, Fairlawn, and Chestnut Courts on the long rectangles of land above the Yacht Club.

In the left front, a dike cuts off the mouth of the creek that winds along what will become the Bimini Waterway The water level has been lowered and work will soon begin pumping in the landfill that will form Butterfield and Firwood Courts and Bimini Avenue at this location.

plant that must be built on Marco. From there 25,000 feet of mains must be laid on the island itself. In addition, a sewage treatment plant must be built and 24,000 feet of sewer pipes installed beneath the ground. Gas pipes must also be laid – 3,000 feet of them.

It was important, given Marco's remoteness, that a showplace hotel be staffed and ready to accommodate overnight guests by January. Even more essential, the administration and sales office must be ready to serve as the information center.

Deltona must also do considerable street building, since there were only two existing public roads. Nine miles must be ready within the few short months allotted.

And, of course, there must be model homes. Company plans called for 10 of them along Tahiti Road, located amid the sandy pine lands in the island's center, a block from the Administration Building. They would be relatively easy to build. The hard part involved the twelve models on Chestnut Court. These were to be placed on a canal connecting with the Marco River. This would involve the construction of the connecting canal and the installation of a seawalls along this portion of the river.

These were the bare necessities that must be completed in six months. At the same time Deltona must begin building a yacht club on the Marco River. Meanwhile, inland, the first nine holes of the golf course must be shaped and an underground irrigation system installed. And, not far away, the shopping center and gas station on S.R. 953 (Bald Eagle Drive), just south of Collier Boulevard should be started in order to be ready when the first residents moved to Marco late in 1965.

Obtaining the Permits

Deltona was somewhat apprehensive about getting permits from the Collier County commissioners, for they had just been burned by the Gulf American Corp., which was developing the gigantic Golden Gate Estates in the midst of the Big Cypress Swamp just east of Naples. Gulf American had started in 1962 and eventually 171 miles of canals and 807 miles of roads would be cut in a grid through the wetlands. The ill-planned canals flowed into the Gulf of Mexico, causing a calamitous loss of water which was responsible for drought and wildfires in the area. Gulf American used severe pressure tactics to rush inexperienced individuals into purchasing worthless plots. The scandal grew so large that Gulf American was eventually cited in congressional hearings which resulted in the Interstate Land Sales Full Disclosure Act of 1968.

Collier County was governed by five commissioners, none of whom were very knowledgeable in the field of large developments. In the beginning they were suspicious of the Deltona people. "Most of those fellows from Miami were sharp," former commissioner Wesley Downey told me. "And they dressed like they meant business. On the other hand, we wore shorts. Why not, that's what people coming to my office expected. They loved our casual, laid-back way of life."

And there was Commissioner A.C. Hancock, a native Floridian who spoke with a southern drawl and owned the eight-unit Blue Heron Motel. When he had run for office three years earlier, it was to unseat a commissioner known to be favorably disposed toward the Collier interests. Feisty and blunt, Hancock was a key commissioner. Later he would run a patrol boat for the county sheriff.

At first Hancock had been skeptical of the Deltona people, but he quickly realized that they were planning a responsible operation that would greatly benefit the county, not one for a fast buck and let the buyer be damned. Hancock, who had been appalled by the Golden Gate Estates development, told me that "when the Mackles came in, it was like a breath of fresh air."

Hancock, as the commissioner who represented Marco (although there were no specific districts assigned), became Deltona's point man. He dealt with Elliott Mackle mainly. "He was a fine gentleman," Hancock remembers, "soft-spoken, easygoing, fun-loving."

Deltona's executives were relieved when they saw that the commissioners did not view them in the mold of Gulf

American (which soon merged with General Acceptance Corp. and later went bankrupt). "We were welcomed with open arms," Vensel recalls. "The Gulf coast people were anxious to develop their area. Before then almost all the expansion had been on the Atlantic side."

The commissioners granted Deltona a sewer and water franchise in July, which enabled them to begin work right away on these vital utilities.

Next, Deltona had to establish the bulkhead line, which was the exterior boundary of the buildable portion of the island. The actual bulkhead would consist of cement slabs surrounding most of the island except the beach on the Gulf. The bulkheads would be laid in five segments as certain portions of Marco were developed. The first section was approved in August and work commenced before the ink was dry.

Rapidly, now, the Florida Land Sales Board granted Deltona's application to sell property on Marco, and the dredge and fill permits sailed through both county and state agencies.

The Army Corps of Engineers

In addition to the county and state, the federal government claimed jurisdiction over the development of Marco. The Army Corps of Engineers, in particular, had concern for any development that might involve a waterway obstruction resulting in some impediment to the movement of defense materials. Since the effect of the Marco project would be to deepen the Marco River (thereby improving its navigation), little objection was anticipated from the Corps.

The only problem was that work in a Corps dredge and fill permit area must be completed within three years. Thus, since Marco was estimated to be a 15-year project, Deltona was forced to divide the island into five sections. Permits would be obtained for each section as it was ready to be developed. At the time this seemed a minor inconvenience.

The Five Permit Areas

The Deltona planners found that Marco Island segmented itself into five rather natural parts running along roadways S.R. 92 and S.R. 953. The first division contained the commercial heart of the development, as well as the yacht club and golf links. The administration/sales office would also be here. It was bordered by the Marco River on the north and east, by S.R. 953 on the west, and by S.R. 92 on the south. To no one's surprise, the Corps granted the permit just shortly after it had been submitted. Indeed, securing the permit was regarded as such a routine matter that Deltona had been working in the area for several months before approval.

The second area concerned the southwest portion of the island around Roberts Bay. S.R. 92 formed the upper border, with Indian Hill on the east and the Gulf of Mexico on the west. A permit would be sought for the Roberts Bay area in 1967.

The third segment involved the northwest part of Marco around Collier Bay. It was a vital link between permit areas one and two and was on the timetable for 1971.

The fourth and fifth areas reached off toward the mainland on either side of S.R. 92. The portion south of S.R. 92 was called Barfield Bay/Blue Hill and that north of the highway was called Big Key. They were scheduled for development in the mid- and late 1970s.

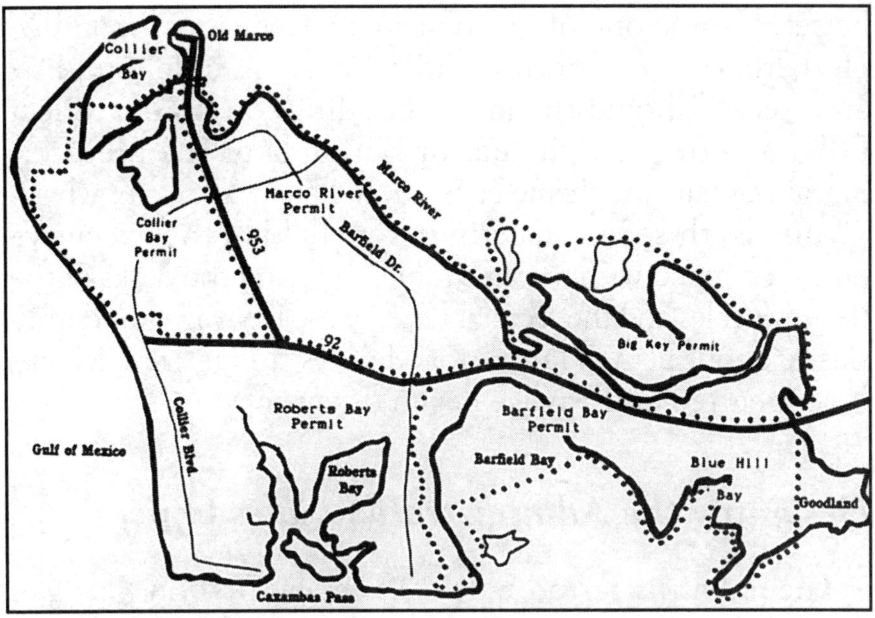

The five permit areas.

Deltona divided Marco into five sections for the purpose of securing dredge and fill permits from the Army Corps of Engineers. Since a permit required that work must be completed within three years of issuance, Deltona was forced to request a separate permit each time it was ready to develop a new portion of the island.

Deltona received a permit for the Marco River area almost automatically on October 27, 1964. After that, different permit areas were designed to be submitted each three years beginning with Roberts Bay then Collier Bay, next Barfield Bay/Blue Hill and finally Big Key.

Of course, there were some portions of Marco that did not require dredge and fill permits. The mid-island, with its low sand hills, was an ideal site just as it was. The coastal area along the marvelous Gulf beach was also perfect without any dredging. Construction in these areas could begin as soon as local regulations were met.

Deciding the Island's Architectural Theme

Before any construction beyond the roads, bulkheads, and utilities could begin, a general theme for Marco had to be set. "It was one of our first major decisions," recalled Herbert Savage, working under Vensel as chief building architect. "Should the major buildings on Marco reflect Polynesia or the Bahamas or Bermuda or the Mediterranean? Should the theme be Spanish, Italian, Greek, or what?" To discuss this issue, meetings were held in the executive office, cramped with a coffee table, sofa, and the desks of the three Mackles and the secretary they shared. Savage was enthusiastic about using Hawaii for Marco's theme. The Mackles concurred and Savage began designing.

Designing the Administration/Sales Office

The Administration/Sales Office was first on Savage's drawing board, since it would be the initial building visitors would be taken to. It must set the pace for all that would follow.

The Mackles had one overriding architectural admonition to Savage: that all the structures he designed for Marco must have wide, glassy entryways that gave a feeling of spaciousness and led the eye through the interior to a beautiful outdoor scene beyond. Keeping this in mind, Savage drew the Administration/Sales Office with wide front doors and a high, Polynesian-style, see-through glass peak above them. Beyond the lobby were glass panels that opened onto an exterior veranda landscaped with sabal palms.

In front of the building Savage placed coconut palms especially selected for their windswept shapes. They would be hauled all the way from Key Biscayne near Miami, for palms were not native to swampy Marco. "We all knew it would be expensive," Savage told me, "but it would be worth it. For everything had to be just right."

Inside the lobby Savage designed large, globular lights to hang down from the high ceiling. In the lobby's center

Deltona's Administration/Sales Office on Opening Day 1965.

This building occupied what was then Marco most prominent location: the northwest corner of S.R. 92 and S.R. 953.

Notice the see-through effect of the Polynesian style lobby. This was a Mackle trademark. The trees were imported from Deltona's development on Key Biscayne just south of Miami. Notice, also, the seabird sculpture on the Marco Island plaque. This became a symbol on Deltona's early advertising material for the carefree living on Marco.

The building, which was abandoned after Deltona fell upon hard times, was torn down in 1992 and a fire station constructed on the site. Nothing was saved except the sea bird, which now resides on the library grounds on South Heathwood Drive.

would be a large table containing a most impressive, three dimensional mock-up of Marco as it would appear when it was fully developed.

The Administration/Sales Office would occupy a large triangular piece of ground where S.R. 92, offering visitors entry from the mainland, met S.R. 953, leading north to the model homes. At the apex of this triangle, as a sort of welcoming salute, Savage placed a12-foot-long decorative stonework with fountains, two high flagpoles, a beautiful sculpture of a seabird in flight, and a graceful red scroll proudly announcing: "Marco Island."

Crescent Beach and the Voyager Hotel.

This photo was probably taken in December 1964. Three Deltona executives have driven onto the beach while discussing future developments. The Voyager, then called the Marco Beach Hotel, had only 50 rooms at this early stage, for its wings and villas have not yet been built.

Notice how soft the sand is. Over the next 2½ decades nearly all this original sand eroded away, and in 1991 an entirely new beach of hard-packed packed shells and other dredging replaced it.

Persons now looking north on this site will be presented with a vista of more than a dozen high-rise condos.

The Voyager Hotel

Savage carried the theme on to the Voyager Hotel (originally named the Marco Beach Hotel), which was assigned a location just south of where S.R. 92 ended at the beach. "The hotel was largely Polynesian," Savage told me. "I used a bamboo treatment around the entrance. The roof was wood shake. Also the grill railings on the second floor were South Pacific. And in the dining room all the posts were encased with coral. The whole west side opened onto the pool. I had a free air grill, as if the hotel was in Hawaii."

The Emerald Beach condominium, 1965.

The Emerald Beach was the island's first high rise. Facing the Gulf, it rose seven stories and contained 48 one- and two-bedroom apartments. Prices ranged from $19,900 to $49,500. It had a gala opening in May 1966, and was virtually sold out by the end of the year.

Land has been cleared for the erection of two more luxury high rises: the Sunset House on the left and the Tradewinds on the right. Saturn Court connects the Emerald Beach with North Collier Boulevard, which is paved only as far as the Voyager Hotel, a short distance to the right. To the right of Saturn can be seen Dandelion, Wintergreen, and a piece of Buttercup Courts.

Of course, there were effects that were strictly American. Like the pitch and putt golf course Savage placed between the hotel and the beach. That idea came from the Key Biscayne Hotel, which the Mackles had built earlier.

The hotel had 50 rooms originally. But, when the inflow of overnight visitors became so much greater than expected, it was expanded to 100 rooms. Savage himself would spend many overnights at the hotel when he was supervising construction.

The Emerald Beach Condominium

Meanwhile down the beach from the Voyager, work was begun on Marco's first high-rise condominium. Although the building would not be completed until mid-1966, it was an instant hit and for several years a landmark on the island. It rose seven stories, quite a height at the time, and boasted a most unique type of architecture that allowed six of the eight apartments on each floor to have ocean views.

In addition to being located right on the beach, it had its own swimming pool and a 50-car garage.

The Great Gold Dig

Late in 1965 Vensel received a phone call from a gold hunter claiming that he had strong evidence that treasure from a sunken Spanish ship was buried on Marco's beach some 200 feet south of the Voyager. Vensel was intrigued, for the publicity value of such a discovery would be immense. Thus he, along with Robert Mackle, flew over from Miami and met the man, with his super-duper, top-secret metal detector – to use Vensel's description.

The device indicated there was metal below, so Vensel and Mackle had a bulldozer erect a sand wall to keep the tide out and they dug down 8 feet. By then water started coming in, so they returned two weeks later with pumps and plywood to line the hole.

They worked until three in the morning, but were still bothered by seepage. Realizing they would need sheet metal and stronger pumps, they decided to abandon the effort until the company got around to putting up the Marco Beach Hotel on the shore behind the beach.

But before they left, they sent a jet lead pipe down more than 20 feet, at which point they heard the distinct

PRICE LIST

Emerald Beach

APARTMENTS

A CONDOMINIUM

UNIT	2nd FLOOR	3rd FLOOR	4th FLOOR	5th FLOOR	6th FLOOR	7th FLOOR
1 & 8	$19,900	$21,000	$22,000	$23,000	$24,000	$25,000
3 & 6	21,000	22,000	23,000	24,000	25,000	26,000
2 & 7	33,000	34,500	36,000	37,500	39,000	40,500
4 & 5	39,500	41,500	43,500	45,500	47,500	49,500

CONVENTIONAL FINANCING TERMS AVAILABLE

MONTHLY OPERATING EXPENSES

APARTMENT UNIT	3 & 6	1 & 8	2 & 7	4 & 5
MONTHLY PAYMENTS	$54.00	$61.00	$90.00	$97.00

Monthly Operating Expense covers insurance, waste collection, water, sewerage, building management and maintenance of the grounds and facilities. Electric and telephone service within each apartment unit and real estate taxes will be billed separately.

MACKLE BROS. DIVISION
Marco Island Development, The Deltona Corporation
Marco Island, Florida

Prices subject to change without notice

Emerald Beach condominium, 1965 price list.

clink, clink, clink of metal on metal. "There is something down there," Vensel told me. "Maybe gold or maybe just a keg of nails – but something."

Deltona never tried again, for the recovery cost was estimated at more than $25,000 and neither Frank nor Elliott Mackle thought the chance of finding real treasure was worth the cost.

Whatever is buried there remains 90 or so feet due west of Quinn's Restaurant beneath the Marriott beach.

The First Homes

When Savage designed the initial 22 homes, he had a certain amount of leeway. "Frank Mackle didn't care so much about how they looked from the outside," Savage recalled. "He just didn't want buyers to walk in the front door and see the kitchen or a living room wall. He preferred that they see through the house to the patio, or the pool, or the waterway beyond."

Frank Mackle also wanted the homes to be small enough to be affordable. There were three models, which could be adapted to suit the desires of the buyer by an architect on location. Two of the models were single story with one-car garages. The third was split level with a two-car garage. They ranged from one bath and one bedroom to three baths and three bedrooms. Prices started at $14,900 for a small inland home and topped out at $41,500 for a large house on a waterway.

The homes had all the latest devices, including air conditioning, which was just coming into use for private residences. They also had gas for cooking, with individual tanks for most homes. The direct gas lines would come later.

Mobilizing a Sales Force

All the planning could be done to perfection, but that would not sell the project. Somehow Marco must be brought to the attention of potential buyers in a way that would impel them to actually put down good money for what at first would be little more than a mangrove wasteland broken by bare sand dredgings and a few stubby canals. What was really being sold was the Mackles' reputation and their promise that Marco would be converted to a marvelous Polynesian paradise in a few short years.

Other developers in Miami thought the Mackles had lost their senses. Marco was too far from anything. The rustic swing bridge that connected it to the mainland was symbolic of its isolation. It was folly for the brothers to dump $4 million construction cash into this swampy wilderness with no real assurance that the public would accept it.

The selling of Marco fell on the shoulders of Neil Bahr. This upbeat, supremely confident man was certain he and his staff could successfully promote Marco. "I felt we had a huge market out there both among retirees and persons who wanted winter homes," he told me. "I knew I could convince many of them that Marco, with its wonderful beaches and miles of waterways, would be a desirable place when we were through."

Nonetheless, even Bahr realized it would be a race against time, since the entire capital of the Marco Island Development Corp. would be exhausted by the grand opening date. "I realized we must generate tremendous sales almost immediately," Bahr confided, "for the initial expenses at Marco were going to be far higher than we had ever experienced before."

Bahr had been given a role which few others would have dared accept. Yet he was not one to shirk challenges. During World War II, he had served on a submarine which sank several Japanese warships. At one time his sub had lost power and sat on the floor of the Java Sea for 20 terrifying hours while repairs were made.

After the war, Bahr became involved with real estate sales in the Cleveland area and soon rose to general manager of the largest residential brokerage firm in Ohio. At this point he attracted the notice of the Mackles, who offered Bahr and his company a franchise to sell their properties in Ohio. After thoroughly checking the Mackles out, Bahr accepted. He was so successful that within a couple of years he had moved to Miami and was working for the Mackles directly.

In anticipation of Marco coming on line, Bahr expanded Deltona's network of franchised agents by nearly 70 percent in 1964. These agents operated out of 63 protected territories, mainly in the northern United States, but also in Western Europe, Latin America, and even the Far East. Bahr selected only the most successful real estate dealerships in each area to handle Deltona properties. They sold their clients lots and new homes mainly sight unseen with the understanding that, if after a personal visit to Marco, the client felt the property had been misrepresented in any way, he could obtain a refund.

This presale program had been a staple Mackle innovation for several years. It enabled a buyer to put either 10 percent down on a lot or merely sign a home purchase contract, then take a chartered plane to Florida with most of the expense paid for by the company and its agents. These flights, which carried as many as 200 persons at a time, were called "Air Caravans" and were originated by Neil Bahr. The program quickly became a major sales tool and helped account for the fact that nearly three-fourths of Deltona's lots and more than half of its homes were presold by franchised agents operating far from Florida.

As the January 31 grand opening approached, Bahr increased the tempo of his preparations. To further stimulate his agents, he arranged for a gala sales convention on

Marco. They were flown down in shifts during the first two weeks of January. They stayed at the Voyager, where, although workmen were still busy, the pool was full and the banquet table was always heaped with tropical delights.

For some agents their first visit to Marco literally changed their lives. One of these was Leonard Llewellyn, born in Montana and destined to become one of Deltona's most successful franchised agents. "I've never been the same since I first saw Marco," Llewellyn told me. "I loved the sand beach and the emerald Gulf. I loved the waving palm trees. Montana has two seasons: July and winter. This was paradise."

The sales conference was a tremendous success and when the agents went back to the frigid North, they conveyed their enthusiasm to their clients. They assured them that the island was being developed just as the Mackles had promised. They had seen the homes being built, the utilities going in, the canals being dug. They were more confident than ever that the Mackles were men of their words.

The agents advised their clients that this was one of south Florida's few remaining undeveloped recreational sites. When it was sold out, there might never be another. It was, in effect, the *Last Paradise*.

Promoting Marco

To proclaim Marco's wonders, Bahr instituted a large promotional campaign during the final weeks before the grand opening. He earmarked $600,000 for a whirlwind of advertising that included full-page spreads along with 12 page color supplements in 30 major newspapers and national magazines both in the U.S. and overseas. In addition, the advertising barrage featured bus placards and highway billboards around the nation. Finally, as the grand opening approached, Bahr bought nearly 700 television and radio spots.

By these means citizens in the freezing January climes learned about "the haunting allure of the South Seas on Florida's Gulf Coast." They became aware that Marco was "the last major tropical island in Florida" and that here Deltona was "creating a mood for living gloriously different than any you've ever known." They found assurance in the Mackles' reputation and their master plan which promised "an orderly building of houses of worship and schools, modern shopping plazas, recreation areas, an 18- hole championship golf course, and a yacht club with complete boating facilities."

The campaign was wildly successful. It stirred a longing held by almost every snowbound person for a place where tropic breezes fanned swaying palms; where tepid surf broke over sunny beaches. A place where one could dine on a private terrace overlooking a waterway more lovely than Venice.

Letters requesting more information began pouring into Deltona's Miami headquarters. Hundreds of them daily. Then thousands. The mail room became stuffed with bag after bag. Extra sorters were hired. Yet still the avalanche of mail tumbled in. The first month alone Deltona received more than 50,000 requests. Even Bahr was astonished.

The Grand Opening, January 31, 1965

At last the big day arrived! The crowds appeared early. Some came by pleasure boat from Naples and other communities up the coast. Others flew in on private planes, landing at the airstrip that had been created out of the road which had led to the now-abandoned Air Force Missile Tracking Station. Many more came by car – some from

Deltona's sales lobby on Opening Day, 1965.

A salesman points out the Chestnut Court model homes on this impressive mockup of Marco. Individual sales offices are down the hall in back of the salesman. The visitors, many still in their northern attire, are part of the Deltona Air Caravan program.

Miami and others from Fort Myers and Orlando. A number were Florida natives, curious to see how the Mackles could possibly have transformed this inhospitable island into anything worth living on. Others were wintering tourists eager to inspect this much ballyhooed locale.

Large numbers arrived by bus across the Everglades from Miami as part of Bahr's Air Caravans. They often came in groups accompanied by the franchised agent who had already sold them property subject to site inspection.

One of the agents on Marco this historic day was Llewellyn. "It was exciting, even electric," he remembered. I had never seen anything like it! Everyone was enthusiastic!"

And why not? The island was festooned with colorful banners. Cars with happy families were everywhere. Deltona employees were stationed at each stopping place with brochures and answers to every question.

The Chestnut Court model homes on Opening Day, 1965.

These, and a similar group of models on Tahiti Road, were the first homes built by Deltona on Marco. Prices started here at $19,800. There are approximately 70 cars in the parking lot and along the road, indicating the popularity of the homes, even though long shadows show it is quite late in the day.

Fairlawn and Buttonwood Courts, above Chestnut, will soon have model homes.

Collier Boulevard runs across the photo, ending at the Marco River. The Yacht Club is on the river. Barfield Drive begins at Collier and continues down the bottom of the photo. Barfield Drive will be extended and homes built on the channel opposite Chestnut. The cement forms for the seawall slabs are already lying as little gray rectangles along the side of the channel.

Visitors usually went to the sales office first. There they gaped over the huge three-dimensional mock-up of the completed island. Sales personnel eagerly described Deltona's plans to turn Marco into a tropical paradise. Neil Bahr, himself, was on the floor.

From the sales office, directional signs pointed visitors to the southern part of the island where they could park on Indian Hill and gain a panoramic view of Marco from a platform which Deltona had carted over from the defunct Missile Tracking Station. For the more adventurous, there was a 20- foot tower that would offer an even loftier vista.

Most visitors wanted to see the model homes next and advertising posters guided them to Tahiti Road, near the sales office. Here were 10 homes neatly lined up on both sides of the street.

Near Tahiti Road was the emerging golf course, with its rolling fairways freshly planted with grass. The first nine holes would be ready within a few months.

But the real highlight was the cluster of 12 model homes on the Chestnut Waterway, just off Collier Boulevard near the Yacht Club. Each had a private backyard overlooking the canal and docking facilities for the pleasure craft it was assumed most Marco inhabitants would purchase.

In order to show prospective buyers Marco's watery environment from a different perspective, Bahr had purchased a vessel, especially built in the South Seas style. It was used to transport up to 40 passengers at a time on scenic tours of the canals, the Marco River, and the Gulf of Mexico. Bahr was very proud of *The Marco Islander*, as the boat was called. It was bright blue and yellow and had a pair of 3-foot Polynesian warrior heads carved on the bow.

Some of the visitors lunched at the Yacht Club, with its elevated terrace overlooking the Marco River. Others wandered into the village of Marco, where they ate at the Marco Inn, some at the same table that the Mackles, Bahr, and Vensel had used on their initial inspection two years earlier.

Most persons simply picnicked at the beach. Deltona had constructed some cabanas made of palm fronds so that it all looked very Hawaiian. Thousands enjoyed the view and romped in the warm water.

The Mackles were at the Voyager much of that day. There they met the most distinguished of the visitors: editors from the North, local bankers, large investors, and, of course, some of the Collier County commissioners. There was a magnificent lunch and an even more incredible dinner.

Early Deltona model homes.

Four representative samples from the 22 models available to buyers on opening day, January 31, 1965.

When it was over, optimism soared at Deltona. The grand opening had been a fantastic success. Bahr estimated that fully 25,000 persons had flocked to Marco this single day alone. They had all been impressed with what they had seen. So word would go out: Marco is all they claim. They were on their way!

4

Creating Beauty Out of the Swamp

The Grand Opening of January 1965 was a milestone. Deltona had shown the skeptics that Marco Island could be sold to the public if it was developed with the care and quality that the company had demonstrated so vividly on opening day.

The Mackle Brothers and Marco Island

The three Mackles were determined that Marco should be Deltona's "showcase community," as they phrased it in an annual report. From the day of its inception, Marco was deep in their hearts and high in their thoughts. The company headquarters in Miami was central control for the island. Neil Bahr operated from there as well, following the Mackles' instructions and putting his sales organization into high gear. All construction orders originated in Miami and from there were communicated to the on-site superintendents on Marco.

The Mackles had a plane circle Marco on a regular basis, from which a photographer took aerial shots of the work in progress. Almost daily meetings were held in the office which the three brothers shared, each brother having a desk in his own corner of the room and visitors seating themselves on the pair of sofas in the fourth corner. Above them

The Mackle Brothers and Neil Bahr present a sales award, 1968.

From left to right: Frank Mackle, Robert Mackle, Leonard Llewellyn, Herman Rock, Neil Bahr, Elliott Mackle.

hovered large oil paintings of Frank Sr., their revered father and founder of the Mackle fortunes, and their mother, Teresa.

There was nothing that escaped the brothers. Each was an expert in construction, and all three had college degrees in engineering. However, they had their own spheres of interest. Elliott had gravitated to the actual construction end, for, as the eldest, he had been most closely involved with their father during the early days. After Frank Sr., died in 1941, Elliott had presided over such important projects as the construction of the Naval Base at Key West. He also had an uncanny instinct for good developmental land.

Robert Mackle, quiet and studious, enjoyed financial matters. As secretary-treasurer of Deltona, he was constantly involved with obtaining the funds that were essential for the company's numerous construction activities. Construction loans usually required the completion of certain phases before funds were released, so Robert was required to make numerous visits to Marco to be sure work was progressing at a satisfactory pace.

Frank Jr., as Deltona's president, was general overseer of the company's operations, which extended over much of Florida. It had been Frank, mainly, who was the catalyst behind the partnership with the Colliers to develop Marco. "I knew from the moment I stood on that wide sandy beach that I wanted to develop Marco," he told me.

At least one of the Mackles made the trip to Marco each week. They would often fly in one of the company's planes, landing at the strip that had been converted from the old Air Force road. They never flew together, for that was an unwritten dictum. "I don't remember such a rule for the other executives," architect Herb Savage told me with a smile. "You know, if they lost the rest of us, the three of them could have run the company alone."

The Mackles conveyed their enthusiasm for Marco to the rest of the Deltona executives. The island presented an irresistible opportunity to create a paradise out of a swamp. Yet there were formidable problems.

The Mosquito Problem

One of the earliest concerns was of controlling the mosquitoes. During the season, the pesky bugs hatched in vast clouds from the marshes that covered so much of the island. Neil Bahr tells the story of a salesman who attended a meeting at the Voyager Hotel. After partying too much, he passed out in the parking lot. When friends discovered him the following morning he was almost completely covered with a voracious mass of mosquitoes who were literally eating him alive. He was rushed to the hospital in Naples, where he recovered.

Frank Mackle recalls standing on the beach during an

early trip to Marco and, when he grasped at the mosquitoes around him, coming up with a fist full of the angry little vampires.

In the pre-Deltona days anyone working outside during the mosquito season had to cover his body with crankcase oil.

Deltona, being more sophisticated, furnished its workers with *Off* spray. "We bought it by the gross: dozens of cases at a time," said C. Edward Hinkley, recalling the days when he was assistant manager for construction and development. "It was one of the largest single items purchased. And it was also the item most stolen by the workers."

The job of relieving the mosquito infestation fell to Jim Vensel. "I went to the Kennedy Space Center," he told me, "because we learned scientists there had done a good job ridding the Canaveral wetlands of the insects." Vensel gathered valuable information. These mosquitoes were of the salt-marsh variety and had an unusual breeding requirement in that they must lay their eggs in soil just dampened by high tide. The eggs remained in the mud until the next high tide washed over them, at which time they hatched. By diking around the breeding areas, then pumping in enough water to raise the level above high tide, the ebb and flow of water upon which the mosquitoes depended would be eliminated and the eggs would not hatch.

When Vensel brought his findings to the Mackles, it was decided that they would use the diking technique at Marco. It was going to be an expensive project, but there was no alternative.

The Mosquito Dikes

The dikes would not have to encircle the entire island. The long sweep of Crescent Beach was bordered with low

Dragline and mosquito dike, 1964.

A dragline digs the Chestnut Waterway. It has piled large mounds of earth, much of which was previously dredged up from the Marco River in the foreground, These mounds will be spread over the land to be occupied by the Yacht Club and Chestnut, Fairlawn, and Buttonwood Courts.

A dike to isolate the area from Marco River tidal ebbs and flows crosses the middle of the photo. It is only about 2 feet above the river level and is embedded with mangrove debris.

dunes which formed their own barrier against the tidal inflows. The land upon which the town of Marco stood was also above the tides. So was the sandy arm forming the Hideaway peninsula and the uplands around both Barfield Bay and the southern portion of Roberts Bay.

This still left a goodly portion of the island which must be diked. In the north the dike began at Magnolia Court and the S.R. 953 embankment. From there it ran along the shore of Marco Bay and extended past Butterfield, Pepperwood, Polynesia, and Stillwater courts then passed the future Blue Hill Court to connect with the elevated roadbed of S.R. 92.

In the south, because the Roberts Bay and Smokehouse Creek lowlands were subject to tidal ebbs and flow, a dike was erected along the upper portion of the bay. It began at the Indian Hills where Barfield and Winterberry Drives now meet. From there it paralleled Winterberry as far as

Heathwood, where it made a long dip into the bay to a point a little past Forrest Court. It then looped upward along Smokehouse Creek before turning south past the tip of Partridge Court. It ended at the point where Shipp's Landing would be built many years later.

The mosquito dikes had to be substantial enough to keep out the insistent push of the Gulf tides. They were around 10 feet wide and 5 feet above the water's surface. To construct them, Deltona brought in their draglines. These draglines consisted of a tall boom with a large bucket at one end of a long cable. The draglines would drop their buckets from a great height, sending them crashing into the shallow water that bordered the Marco River or Roberts Bay. Cables would then drag in the bucket, which scooped up sand, muck, and mangroves. Once full, the buckets would be lifted to the dike's location and emptied.

As soon as enough fill had been deposited in front of a dragline it would move forward on that new land. In this fashion the draglines created their own roadway. Deltona owned a half-dozen of the large draglines as well as many smaller ones. They were extremely versatile and, although early on most were engaged in the erection of mosquito dikes, they were soon moved inland to help dig the canals.

By the end of 1965, with the diking system in place, the mosquito population plummeted. And when a twin engine DC-3 spray plane began running off the Landmark air strip in 1966, the mosquitoes were firmly under control. But they did not vanish completely, and mosquito repellent was still in great demand.

As the development of Marco proceeded, the mosquito dikes were covered with landfill and became the outer edge of the island. Seawalls made them permanent. They now form the base for home lots along the Marco River, Roberts and Collier bays, and many interior waterways.

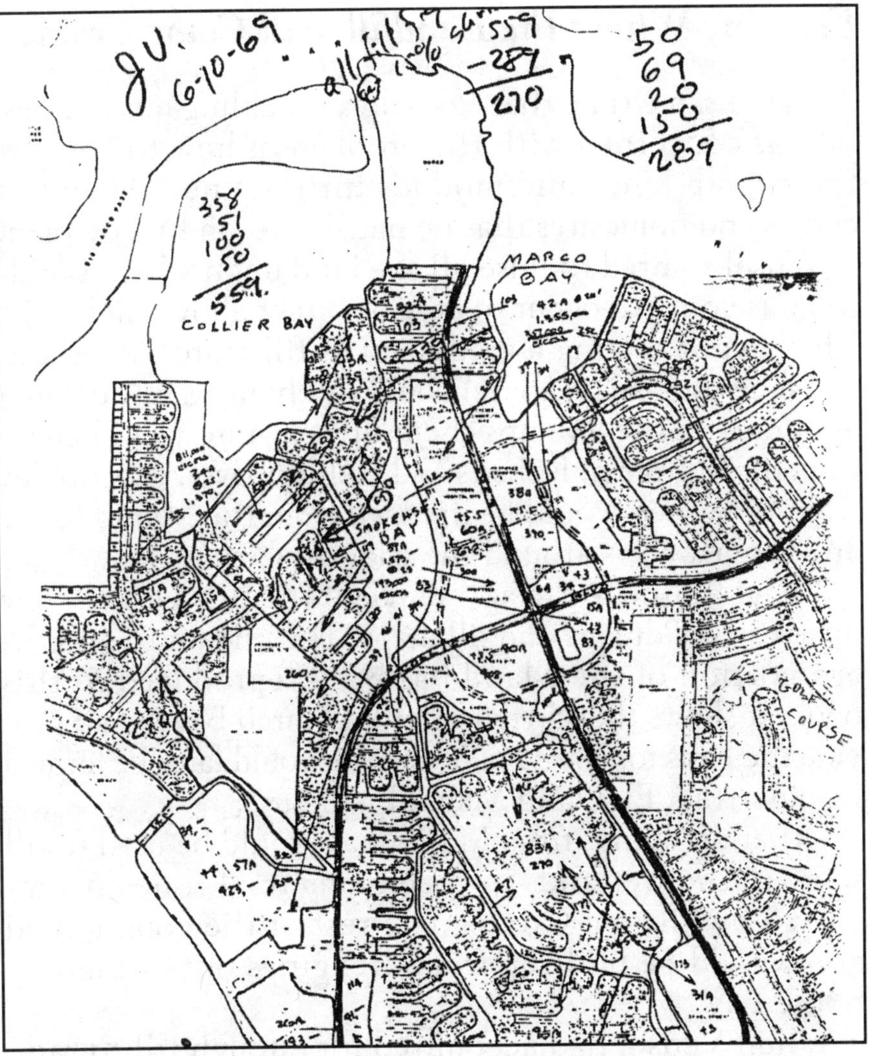

The dredge and fill map.

This map was drawn by Vensel, with his initials and the date of June 10, 1969 at the top. It indicates the sources of the landfill needed to bring the low portions of Marco to 3 feet above sea level.

For example, at Smokehouse Bay Vensel estimated that out of 39 acres dredged to a depth of 25 feet he could obtain 1,573,000 cubic yards of fill material He would have 300,000 cubic yards piped from the right side of the bay, as indicated by the arrow to fill in the marshy ground beyond Elkcam Circle. This area was designed to become the shopping center which now occupies the northwest portion of the town center.

Other Smokehouse dredgings would create the land on the Bay's left side that would be formed into the Crescent, Dorando, and Century peninsulas. When the dredgings from Smokehouse Bay had been distributed to the proper areas, Vensel expected to still have 193,000 excess cubic yards.

Figuring Where the Landfill Will Come From

At the same time that Vensel was tackling mosquitoes, he was concerned with the problem of how to convert the swamps and sand mounds into the neat layout of canals and homesites that he had drawn on his site plan.

Vensel wanted to raise all the land upon which building was going to occur to at least 3 feet above high tide. This meant getting a great deal of fill material. About 60 percent of this material could be obtained by dredging channels in the swamps themselves. More would come from the bottom of Roberts and Collier Bays. And, finally, what remained would be dredged from the Marco River and other waters around the island.

To determine the exact source of the fill, Vensel drew up a series of dredge and fill maps. The one for the northern portion of the island has been reproduced in this book. It shows that dredgings from Marco Bay would provide the basis for the 32 acres which would later be formed into Perrine, Elm, and Magnolia Courts.

Other dredgings from Marco Bay would be used to fill some of the wetlands in the commercial zone encompassed by Elkcam Circle. The rest of the commercial area would be built up from dredgings out of Smokehouse Bay.

When Vensel had accounted for enough fill to raise the land 3 feet above high tide in this portion of Marco, he found he still would have an excess of what he needed. This would be piled up and await use as earthen platforms for the houses as they were built – since each house had to be a foot and a half above street level to ensure drainage.

The "War Rooms"

To accomplish its momentous task at Marco, Deltona mobilized almost like an army on a campaign. Indeed, the war room in Deltona's Miami sales headquarters quickly prickled with charts and maps dotted with moving pins and colored bars which represented the lots completed, the homes ready to be marketed, the sales made, and many other vital facts.

Work moved ahead at an almost frenzied pace. The construction planning and supervision headquarters at Marco was set up, first, on the old Missile Tracking Station, but within a few years just south of the Administration Building between Heathwood and Whiteheart (on a site now occupied by the tennis club). Here six trailers were parked. In one, another "war room" was located. This war room occupied a 15-by-30 foot space and concerned strictly construction procedure. Here construction executives kept track of the work by means of multicolor tapes stuck on a huge 8-by-30 foot wall chart. Of major concern was maintaining maximum utilization of Deltona's equipment, which consisted of bulldozers, loaders, graders, scrapers, draglines, dredges, big pans, backhoes, trenchers, cranes, pile drivers, and a large fleet of trucks. The company's inventory of machinery was so massive that *Professional Builder* magazine believed Deltona to be possibly the largest owner and buyer of residential construction equipment in the entire nation!

Professional Builder was so impressed with the Marco operation that it did a feature article on it. When the magazine's writer visited the war room, there were 10 men at work. Each piece of equipment had been assigned specific locations during the entire year as it was moved between the company's various work sites at Marco or Spring Hill or the town of Deltona or the other operations throughout the state. The magazine writer was further impressed when he

The former U.S. Air Force missile tracking station.

In 1964 Deltona began using the old Air Force buildings as operation central for Marco's construction. The large structure at the left was the Air Force's main computer building. The Deltona Corp. converted it into a huge storage facility in which it housed refrigerators, stoves, wallboards, and most of the other goods used in construction. In the center of the photo is the dark outline of the twin mixing towers. The taller one contains cement; the shorter, sand and gravel.

The sand road leading away from the site will later become Seagrape Drive and Landmark Street.

learned that to aid in the complicated planning, Deltona was using one of those newfangled computers.

Deltona kept its own repair shop at Marco, along with a goodly supply of spare parts. These facilities occupied the former Missile Tracking Station. The government had leased the site and now turned it back to the owner, which was the Marco Island Development Corp. As work moved along, the once high-tech buildings became stocked with refrigerators, ranges, roof tiles, and other items to be placed in the homes as they were completed. The station grounds sported miniature mountains of sand, bituminous, and other materials that would be blended into the asphalt which was heated on location and used to surface the streets as they were formed. Deltona also had its own cement making operation on the Tracking Station grounds.

A dredge.

The cables in front support a cutter resting on the water bottom. Debris from the cutter is sucked up by pumps in the cabin and forced through the long pipe that runs to the mainland. Here the dredgings gush over a selected area until it is raised 3 feet above high tide.

There are twin poles, called spuds, at the dredge's rear. One is lowered, indicating that it has been set into the river bottom. Because the dredge cutter is fixed, movement is accomplished by turning the entire boat with the pole as fulcrum. To turn back, the pole that is down now will be raised and that on the left will be lowered. Thus the dredge will figuratively walk down the river.

The pair of round objects on an antenna above the cabin are sighting targets used by surveying teams on shore to make certain the dredge is operating where it should be.

Digging the Canals

The actual construction began with the arrival of the dredges. Dredges were the mainstays of the fill operation. They consisted of powerful pumps installed on a barge. The pumps were connected to a tube which rested on the river's bottom. This tube was around 3 feet wide and at its snout had a cutter with sharp blades. As the blades chewed into the river bottom, pumps sucked the debris into the tube. The tube ran through the dredge to piping at the rear.

This piping led to the shore, where it could reach up to 1500 feet-or the length of five football fields! When it was running at full capacity, the 14-inch pipe could spew enough material to quickly coat a large area with a squishy conglomeration of dredgings.

The dredgings gushed over the designated areas, washing over weeds and shrubs. They also covered the roots of the mangroves, causing the low trees to die. Once the time came to get rid of them, bulldozers simply knocked them down and buried them in additional landfill. When the dredges were through, the once swampy land in the section being worked on looked like a flat, sandy desert.

Even as the dredges were pouring fill into the work area, teams of surveyors began flagging the routes of the canals that were to be dug. The surveying teams maintained precise control of where the digging went on, for Vensel's plan must be followed minutely.

Hardly had the surveyors finished then draglines began scooping the canals. With dikes keeping out the water, the draglines and other equipment could dig "in the dry." As the canals were dug, the draglines deposited large piles of sand and dirt along the sides. Pan scrapers, bulldozers, and front-end loaders then distributed this fill over the surface of the land, raising it to 6 feet above high tide.

The landfill which was laid down in this fashion was not of a proper consistency for homes to be built on it. Before construction Deltona did test borings into the subsoil. Based on these tests, reinforced concrete pilings were driven into the soil to a depth of up to 25 feet. To provide support for an average home, some 20 of these long posts would be needed.

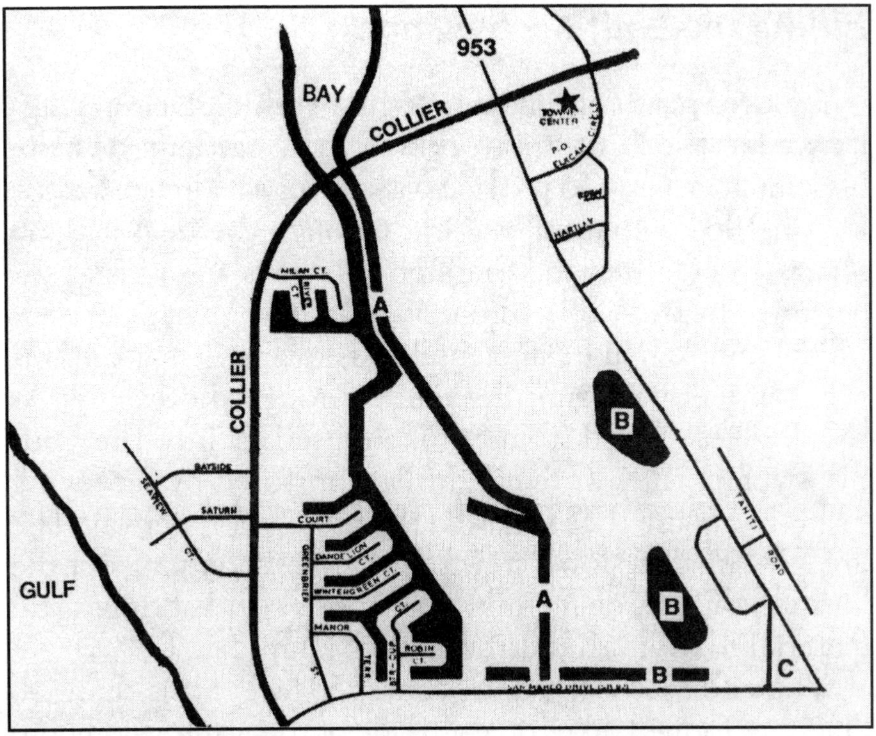

Developing the Unit Six swamp, 1965-66.

For construction purposes, Deltona divided Marco into work units. Unit Six encompassed the large swamp that existed in the triangle between North Collier Boulevard and S.R. 92 and S.R. 953.

Draglines first erected dikes to demarcate the main channel shores. Next dredges, floated in from Smokehouse Bay, began digging this channel, which ran along the future West Joy Circle and Edgewater Court, then turned to parallel what would be Copperfield Court. As the dredgings filled the swamp west of the dikes, draglines and bulldozers, digging canal beds in the dry, formed the fingers of land that became such streets as Manor, Robin, Buttercup and shortly later Milan and River Courts.

Street formation started in the extreme southwest corner of Unit Six in 1965 because this area was most visible to prospective buyers visiting the Emerald Beach Condominium and Voyager Hotel nearby.

To control mosquitoes, a dike was built across the remaining swampy area (letters A on the map). This dike started at the S.R. 92 embankment and ran north between Olive and Cottonwood Courts, then along Edgewater Court to the Collier Boulevard embankment.

Deltona also used other portions of Unit Six for borrow pits (letters B on the map). Two ran along S.R. 92. But a pair of larger ones were formed just west of what became Waterway Drive and between Strawberry, Capistrano and Wales Courts. The material dug from these pits was used to fill the marshy land for the first homes along Tahiti Road and for the initial shopping strip on S.R. 953 just south of Elkcam Circle. These two pits, now filled with water, still exist as part of the inland canal system.

Deltona's island headquarters was at the corner of S.R. 92 and S.R. 953 (letter C).

Filling the Unit Six Swamp

The area south of Smokehouse Bay, which Deltona designated as the Unit Six work zone, was particularly troublesome to access. To provide passage for the dredge barges, late in 1964 a channel was cut through the neck of land separating Collier and Smokehouse bays at a point now occupied by the Collier Boulevard bridge.

From Smokehouse Bay Vensel had designed a major waterway 150 feet wide running south through the swamp. As the dredges moved from Smokehouse Bay into the Unit Six swamp, they were carefully monitored by surveying teams to be sure they followed the proposed waterway. The dredges churned slowly down the center chomping out the bottom, thereby deepening the channel while bringing up material to fill in the surrounding swamp.

While dredges worked the center 50 feet of this channel, draglines formed dikes on each side of the waterway. Then, moving forward on the dikes they themselves had erected, they scooped out the 50 feet on either side of waterway. Most of the landfill for this area (bordered by S.R. 92 and S.R. 953 and North Collier Boulevard) came from these channels. The remainder was dredged from the bottom of Smokehouse Bay.

Erecting the Seawalls

Once the land had been raised and the channels dug, Deltona was ready to erect the seawalls.

By the time this stage was reached, water had usually percolated through the earthen dikes which separated the canal work areas from the exterior water. If this was the case, in order to lower the water, deep pits were dug on the land side of the dike. Water from the canals drained into them

Seawall Installation.

This canal separates Buttonwood, on the right, from Fairlawn, on the left. The waterway connecting with the Marco River runs across the top of the photo, where its course can be followed by the row of dirt pilings, which later will be leveled to form Martinique Court.

The seawall slabs have just been set in place. A few of the rods which anchor the slabs to 3-feet-by-3-feet, "dead men" cement blocks can be seen at the bottom left of the photo. The forms for the wall's cap are in place, with the U-shaped supports securing them to the seawall slabs. The cement will soon be poured into the forms. Two wooden chutes lay ready for use in the foreground.

and was pumped outside over the dike. The canals did not have to be drained completely in order to install the seawalls.

The seawalls were composed of large cement slabs 4 to 5 feet wide and 12 feet long. They were vital to protect the shore from erosion.

The slabs were cast right on location by trucks carrying cement from the mixing facility at the old Missile Tracking Station. The wall forms were laid on the ground, reinforcing rods were put in place, cement was poured and, when it had hardened, the slabs were lifted by draglines and lowered to the bottom slope of the canal floor.

When the slab rested on the bottom, it was not yet secure. To embed it, workmen directed long, thin pipes called jet leads against the mud at the base. The jet leads shot water under extremely high pressure. As the jet of water forced the mud away, the slab sank of its own weight until it reached a position 8 feet below the level of the water when the channel was filled.

Once a slab was in place, a rod 20 feet long was attached to its interior side. The rod reached back into the canal bank where it was connected to a cement block about 3 feet by 3 feet called a "dead man." The rod and the "dead man" were buried under several feet of earth and served to tie the seawall to the land.

The last step consisted of capping the seawall. This involved placing plywood forms over the top of the slab and pouring in a layer of cement.

Developing the Town Center

From the beginning James Vensel had designated the junction of S.R. 953 (Bald Eagle) and the roadway he called Collier Boulevard to be the island's commercial center. It was then used as a landing site for ducks and alligators from Smokehouse Bay who roamed as far inland as the future site of McDonald's restaurant. Vensel wanted scheduled landfill to be dredged in principally from Smokehouse Bay. The problem with this plan was that Smokehouse was part of the Collier Bay work area, and Deltona would not apply for the Army Corps of Engineers dredge and fill permit until several years hence. Therefore Deltona concentrated its first efforts on what it called the "initial shopping center."

The initial shopping center was constructed on the land between S.R. 953 and Tallwood Street just south of Elkcam Circle. This area, too, tended to be wet so a large U-shaped

Marco's business section in late 1966.

This photo looks north up Bald Eagle (S.R. 953) to Collier Boulevard, which crosses from left to right. This is now Marco's commercial district.

The upside down U-shaped object is a borrow pit dug by Deltona to provide landfill for the area to the south. The pit is now the parking lot for the Town Center Mall

Elkcam Circle bends across the upper right of the picture. It has not yet been extended to the west, which is mainly a thick mangrove swamp. The abandoned road between Old Marco and Caxambas arches northward through the mangroves, passing a barely visible clearing of the early settler's cemetery on its left.

Six buildings line Bald Eagle. From north to south they are: 1. the not-complete restaurant with its parking lot still unpaved; 2. the tiny post office; 3. the strip shopping center with a 7-Eleven store and a Z-shaped sidewalk shade-roof; 4. the Gulf Oil service station; 5. an unfinished apartment which Deltona is building for an investor from Pittsburgh; and 6. a 16-unit, two-story apartment building, the first constructed on Marco.

The dog leg street running between Bald Eagle and Elkcam Circle is Tallwood Street. The cross street is Hartley Avenue. At the intersection of Hartley and Tallwood is another apartment building. This was built to house employees of the Marco Beach Hotel (now the Voyager). Very faintly seen just above Hartley running left from Tallwood, is Eden Court. Eden dead-ends at another apartment for hotel employees. Two other employee apartments are going up on the north side of Eden. These apartments are ten units, two stories and were priced at very low rents to the workers .

The old construction road can barely be made out crossing Hartley where it splits into an upside down Y-shape.

Excavating the marina's docking area, 1966.

A dike separates the excavation from Marco Bay. Pumps have removed the water to 12 feet below sea level. Seawalls have been installed A portion of the seawall is embedded in the sloping land that helps stabilize the structure. This is a characteristic of all Marco's waterways.

The flat platform jutting across the center of the photo is a pier. The wooden poles around the pier will be mooring pilings. This work is being done "in the dry." Notice the heavy truck behind the pier.

When the area is complete, the dike will be removed by draglines and the basin filled with water.

borrow pit was dug on the location of what would be the regional mall's south wing. Landfill was hauled from the pit across Elkcam to the initial center. The earliest buildings to go up were a strip shopping center of five units and a service station. The first tenant in the strip was a 7-Eleven grocery. "We always put in a 7-Eleven convenience store when we started developments," said Bahr, who handled those matters for Deltona. "It gave the new residents a sense of well being. We enticed the 7-Elevens by giving them ridiculously low rents – like one percent of gross sales."

Later in 1965 other tenants joined 7-Eleven, including a hardware store and a beauty parlor/barber shop. The same year Deltona had built a small post office just north of the strip shops.

Gulf Oil occupied the service station. As for choosing Gulf Oil, there was no debate. The Collier family had the Gulf franchise.

In early 1967, the island got its first eating establishment: an 88- seat restaurant north of the post office. Deltona itself ran the restaurant for several years. At about the same time the company constructed a medical facility on Elkcam Circle. Bahr sold the structure to Dr. Arthur Cox, who provided the islanders with service for many years.

Meanwhile Deltona was building a marina on a 5-acre site over on Marco Bay. The important fact about the marina was that a group of private businessmen had researched the island and decided it was a good investment. It opened with great fanfare early in 1967.

5

THE FAIR WEATHER YEARS, 1965-67

As 1967 drew to a close, Deltona had ample reasons to be proud of the past and confident of the future. "For the fifth consecutive year," Frank Mackle told his stockholders, "the Deltona Corporation achieved new highs in sales and earnings."

The Gains Start Pouring In

Marco was of special significance. Although company sales were going quite nicely at the other sites, chiefly the town of Deltona, near Orlando, and Spring Hill, near Tampa, in just three years home sales on Marco had soared to $3.5 million or a third of Deltona's total. Land sales were even higher: nearly $11 million, at an average of around $10,300 per lot.

Deltona stock prices reflected the confidence of the investment community. Whereas stock had been selling for $12 per share in 1963, by the end of 1967 it was up to nearly $20 representing a rise of 40 percent. And why shouldn't the stock go up, for Deltona was earning a fat after-tax profit of more than 12 percent!

One reason for Marco's sudden takeoff was that the homes sold at an average price of $28,000, more than twice the price at other sites. Marco was putting Deltona in a new

Looking north from Windmill Avenue in 1966.

The Marco River is on the right, with Smokehouse Bay at the upper left, Collier Bay at the extreme upper middle, and Marco Bay at the upper right. Barfield Drive runs diagonally from left to right. Above it on the left is the golf course, with the bunkers forming short, light colored lines.

Windmill Avenue runs across the bottom, with Pepperwood, Balsam, and and Tarpon Courts branching out from it right to left. The next projection of streets are formed by Bimini as the main stem, with Butterfield and Firwood branching from right to left. Antilles, Goldcoast, Tripoli, Bamboo, and Waikiki form thumbs of land between the peninsulas.

Pepperwood and Balsam are still connected by a wide dike. The water in the landlocked area has been lowered by pumping it out which can be seen at the bend of the water "L".

The seawall slabs have been cast and lay on both sides of the interior canal.

At the bottom of the photo, the seawalls are already in place. The tie-back rods have been installed and the grooves are visible where they will connect with the "dead men" stabilizing blocks.

field, one of higher profitability.

And the best apparently was to come. In 1967, Deltona broke ground for the Sea Breeze and the Sea Breeze, South, a pair of low-rise condo complexes near the Emerald Beach back from the water. Both sold-out three weeks after being put on the market– before they were even completed. And the Sunset House, a high-rise condo on the beach, was barely started when it had sold half its 90 units at an average price of $30,000.

By the end of 1967, Deltona was also far along in its plans to build the major shopping center at the southeast corner of Collier Boulevard and S.R. 953 (Bald Eagle).

Just as exciting was the news that state bonds would soon be issued to pay for construction of a five-story-high bridge to connect Marco with the mainland via North Collier Boulevard. Building would start in the spring of 1968.

The Glories of the Country Club

But the shopping center took a back seat to what the Mackles deemed an even higher priority. This was the Marco Island Country Club. Golf was a sport the Mackles were personally close to. They also felt that, with an island as isolated as Marco, a major recreation facility was required. Accordingly, Herbert Savage was given the assignment of designing a unique clubhouse. This he did by creating five, peak-roofed buildings connected by open-air covered walkways.

"I designed it as a Polynesian village," Savage explained to me. "We had cedar wood shakes on the roofs, which was the closest to representing the natural materials they used in the Pacific. You entered the club through a bamboo gate into a screened courtyard. All the walkways were screened in the original, before we had control of the mosquitoes.

"One of my main objects in having the five original buildings was to permit the expansion we all knew would come. There are nine buildings now. One of my greatest compliments came after we built the four additional units a half-dozen years later. Someone said, 'why, the new club house looks just like the old one.' It did, too, except that it was more than twice as large!"

The front nine holes were opened in 1966 and the back nine soon thereafter. By the next year an annual national tournament was begun. It was an instant success. Celebrities from a wide range of fields attended. Many formed strong friendships with the Mackles. Among these celebrities

An aerial view of the golf course looking southwest.

The clubhouse, comprised of a cluster of Polynesian-style units, is in the center foreground. Nassau Court is in front. Shadow Ridge Court crosses the golf course, ending at a triangle of land formed by Majorca Circle and Society Court. It was here that the ancient railroad had its turn-around.

Bayport Avenue heads west from the old turnaround to end at Bald Eagle Drive. One block before Bald Eagle is Tahiti Road, where the first homes built on Marco are clearly discernible.

Beyond Bald Eagle is the old Unit Six swamp. Such streets as Strawberry, Capistrano, and South Seas are just rising out of dredgings from the swamp. Above them is Deltona's second temporary landing strip, a straight, narrow line running across most of the photo's upper portion.

Above the airstrip, also just created out of the swamp is Copperfield Court with its short appendages such as Ivory, Snowberry and Beaver.

were Lee Trevino, Don Shula, Joe Namath, Mickey Mantle, Jackie Gleason, Perry Como, and Richard Nixon.

Each of the Mackle brothers would try to get in a game of golf whenever he visited Marco, which was as often as once a week. Perhaps Robert Mackle played the most frequently. The most reserved of the three, he may have sought relief from his duties as secretary-treasurer and his endless negotiations with the banks. Yet, ironically, banking friends were often his guests on the links.

Expansion at the Voyager Hotel, 1965

The hotel had hardly been built when Deltona found that the influx of visitors was even greater than expected and that the facilities must be expanded. Here, the dining room is made larger. Meanwhile, two new wings are being added, doubling the number of rooms to 100.

Conventioneers Find the Voyager Hotel

The popularity of the golf course was certainly at least partially responsible for the fact that the Voyager Hotel was exceeding even the most optimistic expectations. It now had 100 rooms spreading in a V-shape to embrace a large pool which overlooked the nine-hole pitch and putt golf course and the famous Crescent Beach beyond. Forty-four luxurious villas flanked the golf course. So great was the Voyager's appeal that many of America's largest corporations began seeking it out for conventions. By 1967 sales were nearly a million dollars – a rise of 23 percent from the prior year. And bookings for the first 3 months of 1968 were a full 70 percent ahead of 1967!

The demand was so great that the Mackle brothers began planning a second beachfront hotel just south of the Voyager. This hotel would be three times larger than the Voyager!

Foreshadow of Doom

Frank Mackle's crystal ball was rosy. This was just the beginning. "We have developed the tools we need for continued expansion," he wrote in the annual report of 1967. "We are in an excellent position to make aggressive moves that in future years will both broaden the scope of our activities and increase their profitability."

Yet even as the cheery news flowed in, Deltona was engaged in practices which would ultimately prove its undoing. Foremost was its vaunted Coordinated Growth Plan.

The Coordinated Growth Plan was devised by Bahr. The concept was brilliant. It was going to take a tremendous amount of money to develop such a primeval location as Marco Island. If Deltona had to borrow these funds, the interest would be so great that the price of land and homes would be almost prohibitive to sales. On the other hand, there were many persons who would want to purchase homesites for future use but lacked the money for an all cash sale. Hence – Bahr's Coordinated Plan.

According to this plan, Marco was divided into five areas depending on when they were scheduled to be developed. The land in the Plan Area I would be ready in three years. Thus a person could put a small amount of cash down and pay for the rest in modest monthly assessments over the three years. Homesites in other plan areas could be financed over longer times, with land out on Barfield Bay and Big Key extending to eight and a half, and later to 10 years,. As for the prices, waterfront lots in 1964 sold for between $5,500 and $16,000 and lots not on water began at $2,550.

As this plan started to function, Deltona began receiving regular monthly payments at 5 percent interest for land still in the raw state! The money coming in was used to develop current properties, thus saving bank expenses. When the time arrived to deliver the land, it would be financed by sales in the areas previously developed. Marco, in effect, became a huge money machine.

The Coordinated Growth Plan went into effect right from the beginning. Lots far out in the wilderness were sold to eager buyers, many of whom found that the monthly payments were less than the land's appreciation. Ninety-five percent of the land sales were made under the plan.

No buyer suspected anything could go wrong. After all, Deltona owned the land and the Mackle brothers' record of fulfilling their promises was impeccable. Of course, there was the matter of dredge and fill permits, but that appeared to be minor, for hadn't the Army Corps granted the first of the required five permits in a manner that could only be called perfunctory?

The buyers' contracts and notes receivable took on a life of their own. There were almost no defaults, for the rising land prices at Marco brought a far better return than stocks. Even normally wary banks, such as the First National of Boston, began accepting the notes as collateral for loans made to Deltona. This could only be viewed as sound business if everyone was certain the notes' monthly payments would be met to maturity. The only reason such payments would not continue was if there was doubt in the buyers' minds that Deltona would, or could, not deliver the land in a fully developed condition at the end of the purchase period as promised. Frank Mackle was elated. "It reflects [our] increasingly sound financial stature," he told his stockholders.

Enter an Unforeseen Adversary: The Environmentalists

Yet the Mackle brothers were unknowingly building a delicate house of cards. They, and almost everyone, assumed there would be no problem delivering the promised property with the land elevated, the swamp gone, canals dug, and roads in place.

But events beyond the Mackles' control were unfolding. In the mid-1960s the environmental movement began to stir. Deltona was quick to recognize it and adopted what were very progressive responses for the time. Comments from governmental officials in the regulatory agencies about the company's operations ranged from "a fine cooperative spirit" to "a farsighted recognition of the values of fish and wildlife resources."

Deltona did not suspect anything would interfere with its plans when on September 20, 1967, it routinely applied to the Army Corps of Engineers for a permit to dredge and fill around Roberts Bay, the second of its five permit areas.

6

THE BATTLE FOR ROBERTS BAY, 1967-69

Originally Deltona had not viewed the role of the Army Corps of Engineers as a problem. The Corps was governed by the venerable Rivers and Harbors Act of 1899, which allowed it jurisdiction over only those dredge and fill projects which might interfere with navigational waterways. Navigational waterways were further defined in the 1953 Submerged Lands Act as those covered by non-tidal waters. Thus when Deltona began operations at Marco, the only portions of the island subject to Corps permit requirements were those bordering the Marco River and the bays: Roberts, Collier, and the lower portion of Barfield, which were permanently covered with water.

The first permit, which concerned the northeast portion of the island along the Marco River, was granted routinely four months after submission in 1964. When Deltona's application to develop the second area around Roberts Bay was submitted to the Corps in September 1967, no problem was expected. Indeed, under Deltona's Coordinated Growth Program, a certain percent of the swampy lots in this permit area had already been sold and the company was contractually obligated to deliver most of them in buildable condition within the next three years.

A New Role for the Department of the Interior

In addition to the Corps of Engineers, Deltona had to deal with the Department of Interior's Fish and Wildlife Service, for a later federal act had decreed that the Corps must consult with the Service about the environmental impact of any dredge and fill permit it was considering. Although the Service had only an advisory capacity, the Corps gave much weight to its evaluation of the projects put before it. For this reason Deltona took great pains to cultivate the approval of the Service.

In the beginning, the Fish and Wildlife Service responded very well to Deltona's operations. In a letter written in October 1964, the Service commended Deltona for its responsible development of Marco and even suggested that the company communicate its story to the magazines and conservation organizations.

The main concern of Fish and Wildlife at this time was merely the protection of the eagles' nests which were scattered about Marco. For this purpose Deltona established the entire island as an eagle sanctuary under the auspices of the Florida Audubon Society. Another concern was the preservation of a trio of small Marco River islets used for nesting by thousands of birds in the area. Deltona had originally earmarked these islands to be dredged away for landfill. Instead the company voluntarily set them aside as a permanent conservation preserve to be deeded to the Audubon Society as soon as mortgage requirements permitted.

The spirit of cooperation was everywhere during the early years. Far from opposing Deltona's first dredge and fill application, the Fish and Wildlife Service's report to the Corps of Engineers was most favorable.

The Environmental Movement Begins

But between the submission of the first permit application in 1964 and the second for Roberts Bay in 1967, the climate had begun to change. Something new was in the wind and it was called environmentalism. No longer were conservationists willing to sit passively by while developers uprooted land which was not only beautiful in its natural state but was the home of plants and animals that might be essential for human survival. In 1965 New York environmentalists won an historic court case, called the Scenic Hudson, in which they prevented Consolidated Edison from building a large electric power facility on the river. This was one of the very earliest victories for environmentalism and sent a clarion call throughout the nation.

Among those heeding the call were officials of the Fish and Wildlife Service. They assumed a far more critical view of Deltona's activities on Marco. They began to feel that conservation required more than the posting of a few eagle preserve signs and setting aside three tiny islands in the Marco River as bird sanctuaries.

Influenced by Fish and Wildlife, the entire Department of the Interior grew concerned with the Corps' apparent disregard of conservationist issues. Therefore, the Interior sought to raise the level of its role in the issuance of dredge and fill permits. Thus in July of 1967, at the Interior's urging, the Corps agreed to a Memorandum of Understanding that required a full-scale review at the highest levels in Washington concerning any dredge and fill permit of which the Interior did not approve.

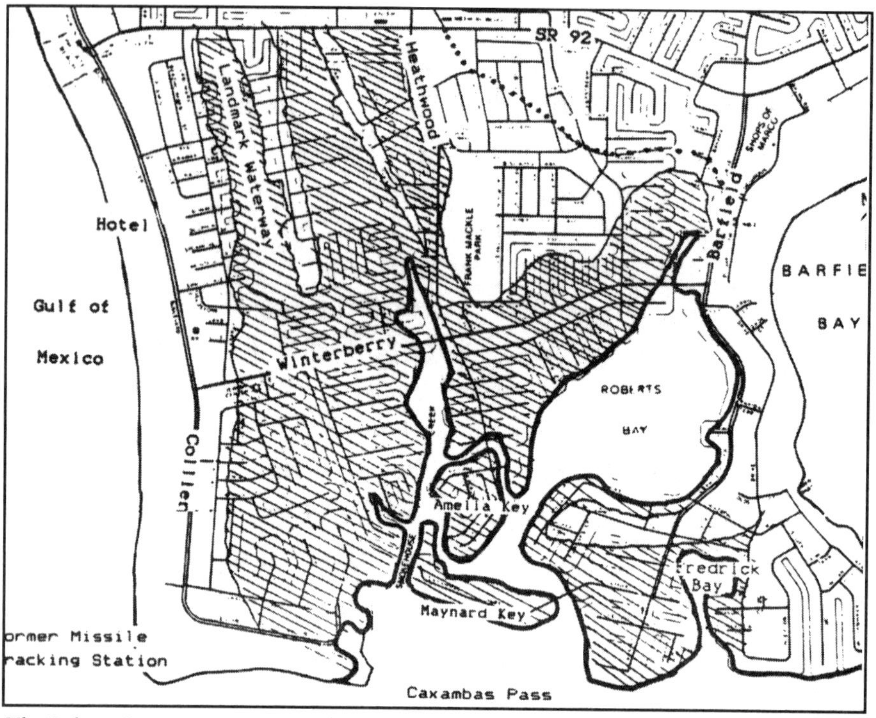

The Roberts Bay permit area in 1968 showing the swampy portion requiring landfill.

The locations that were swampy and needed fill material are indicated by hatching.

Deltona called these Soil Disposal Areas. Some of the fill will come from dredgings in the Landmark Waterway, but most must come from Roberts Bay and Smokehouse Creek and required the approval of the Army Corps of Engineers. A large portion of these lots had already been sold for future delivery.

Landmark Street borders the swamp on the west. It was once part of the old Air Force road leading to the missile tracking station. Landmark would later become Deltona's first airstrip. Heathwood Drive (site of the Collier County Public Library) runs along the swamp's eastern edge.

Two slivers of land protrude into the swamp. The one on the left will become the site of Lamplighter Drive and that on the right the site of Whiteheart/Treasure Courts.

In 1968 the only roads in this area were S.R. 92, Collier Boulevard, and the Old Marco to Caxambas Road, which is dotted in.

The Battle Begins for the Roberts Bay Permit

For these reasons, by the time that Deltona submitted the application for its second permit area, Roberts Bay, the situation had changed radically.

Deltona expected approval to be granted within a few months, as had the first permit. But now, with the Fish and

Wildlife Service scrutinizing Marco far more closely than before, 1967 came and went with no decision

As 1968, too, wore on without a permit, the company began to grow nervous. Five million dollars of contracts under the Coordinated Growth Plan required that large swampy areas around Roberts Bay be filled and delivered to the purchasers by the coming year. This would necessitate the pumping into the area 600,000 cubic yards of fill, much of which could not be obtained without Corps approval.

The Saga of the Landmark Waterway Dredge

Work in a certain portion of the Roberts Bay area did not need a Corps permit. This area included the large Unit Seven swamp, bounded by S.R. 92, South Collier, South Heathwood, and Winterberry. Operations here had started in 1967.

Once in the Unit Seven swamp, the dredge sucked huge amounts of material from the bottom and deposited it in three areas. The first was along the swamp's western edge, where it formed such short projections as Tulip, Birch, and Aster Courts. At the same time the aircraft landing strip was converted into Landmark Street (at which time a new landing strip was opened in the Unit Six swamp along what would become Edgewater Court). On the eastern edge of the swamp a second series of landfill courts was created running off Heathwood. These included Shenandoah, Whiteheart, Mistletoe, and Treasure. Finally, in the middle of the swamp, dredgings were poured onto a finger of pre-existing, semi-dry land to form Lamplighter Court and its appendages such as Coronado, Lighthouse, and Driftwood courts.

By Autumn 1968 the land contract requirements had been met in the former swamp, and Deltona wished to move the dredge into other areas requiring attention. It would seem a simple matter to dig a channel south so the dredge could exit into Roberts Bay. But the Corps, under prodding from the Department of the Interior, now declared that its jurisdiction covered not only navigable water but the shorelines of this water and waterways leading to the shoreline.

Under these new rules, the Corps denied Deltona the right to cut a channel south to permit the dredge to leave the Landmark area. Neither would the Corps permit Deltona to send the dredge back north the way it had come and exit through the channel it had made (and since plugged up) to Collier Bay. The dredge was effectively bottled up and useless. To make matters worse, Deltona was renting the dredge for $3,300 per day!

Deltona wrote the Corps about the "dire emergency" relating to the dredge and the fact that the exit channel would pass through a mainly swampy area that had no value in terms of navigable waterways. The Corps finally relented and Deltona dug south from the Landmark Waterway to where Winterberry Drive would be constructed, and then followed the future Heathwood until the dredge exited into the Roberts Bay channel between Forrest and Quintara Courts. It had taken28 days to complete this simple act and had cost Deltona $92,400 in unnecessary rental payments.

The Run-In Over Fredrick Bay

Deltona was now desperate to complete its obligations under the Coordinated Growth contracts. The state had long ago approved its bulkhead lines, which set the parameters for the island and along which the mosquito dikes had been built. Because hitherto the Corps had jurisdiction only over the navigable waters outside of the bulkhead lines and because Deltona owned outright all the territory within the bulkhead lines, the company believed it had the right to begin digging the slips and waterways within the bulkhead line. Accordingly, the now-released dredge was put to work in Fredrick Bay, a small, virtually landlocked swamp at the extreme southeast tip of the island.

This caused a run-in with the district Corps agent, who inspected the area via helicopter late in August 1968. He warned that the Corps now considered such activities illegal and that in performing them Deltona opened itself to prosecution. The company had no choice except to stop work at the site, sealing the mouth of the waterway with an earthen plug.

The Bombshell

The long delay in granting the Roberts Bay permit, which by this time had reached a year, was caused mainly by the interjection of the Department of the Interior's Fish and Wildlife Service into the approval process. The Service had cooled toward Deltona to the point where it did not even return the company's phone calls. This caused Deltona a great deal of apprehension. And well it might for on September 13, 1968 the Interior's long-awaited decision came. It recommended that the Army Corps deny Deltona's request for a dredge and fill permit for the Roberts Bay area.

The denial recommendation was in the form of a 3½-page letter written by W. L. Towns, acting regional director of the Fish and Wildlife Service. In it he described the diverse flora and fauna that would be destroyed or greatly reduced if Deltona pursued its designs. The area was rich in nutrients that supported life far beyond its immediate environs, Towns contended. The destruction of the red mangroves, in particular, with their intricate root systems sifting though the intertidal margins was unacceptable. Interior felt that, by allowing Deltona to continue, injuries would be caused to commercial fishing, sports fishing, and a variety of recreational activities from bird-watching to picnicking.

When Deltona officials learned of the Interior's recommendation for denial, they were shocked. Towns' letter fell on company headquarters "like an unforeseen bombshell," to use Vensel's words. Numerous strategy meetings were held to determine the company's response. Since the Department of the Interior's recommendation did not obligate the Corps to accept it, for the Corps was part of the Department of Defense and not under Interior's jurisdiction, Deltona directed its efforts to convince the Corps that Interior's concerns were unfounded.

On October 1, 1968 Vensel dispatched a lengthy letter to the Corps defending Deltona's activities at Marco. In it he quoted from Towns himself, who four years earlier had commended Deltona for its "farsighted recognition of the values of fish and wildlife resources." Vensel pointed out that the company's damage to the environment around Marco was minimal. Deltona had always worked closely with Fish and Wildlife, and he thought it unfair that the agency suddenly took the position "that if so much as a shovel of dirt is turned on the bottom of a bay, it adversely affects conservation within the area." He also reminded the Corps that Deltona's operations "will in no way adversely affect or obstruct the navigable capacity of any waters."

The matter continued on into 1969. While much of Deltona's fleet of earth-moving equipment was forced to sit idly by, the Corps vacillated between Deltona's persuasive arguments and the influence of the Department of the Interior. Frank Mackle and Vensel secured a meeting with

Florida senators Spessard Holland and George Smathers in August at which time they agreed to aid Deltona.

In an effort to get Interior to end its opposition, Sen. Holland, an influential man from his position on the Appropriations Committee, sent a long letter to Russell Train, under secretary of the Interior. In it he reminded Train that he himself had admitted that the dredging operations at Marco represented only a "minute destruction of natural habitat." The senator suggested that perhaps the Interior's actions were arbitrary in singling out Deltona when that company had not only tried to act with environmental responsibility, but had already invested great sums in the project based on assumptions valid at the time of investment.

Train's reply was a blunt reiteration of the Department's opposition to granting further permits for work on Marco.

Buried Alive

While Deltona's position at Marco continued to deteriorate, the Mackle family was hit with a tragedy of potentially shattering proportions. Robert Mackle's daughter, Barbara, had been kidnapped!

Barbara and her mother were staying at a motel in northeast Atlanta while Mrs. Mackle was visiting the 20-year-old young woman at Emory University, where she was a student. At four in the morning of December 17, 1968 there was a banging at the door by two persons claiming to be police. When the Mackles opened the door, they were accosted. Mrs. Mackle was chloroformed and bound and Barbara was driven off.

The kidnappers took Barbara, still in her red-and-white checkered nightgown, to a deserted woodland twenty miles northeast of Atlanta and forced her to lie in a coffin-like box. The lid was lowered and screwed in place, then the kidnappers buried the box in the freezing soil. Her only contact with the outside world was through vent pipes.

Barbara lay in the cramped, black box for more than three days. She sang songs and prayed to keep up her courage. And she knocked against the lid with her knuckles, hoping against hope that someone would hear the pathetically weak sound. But she did not give up, for she had utter faith that her father would release her.

Meanwhile her father, mother, uncles Frank and Elliott, as well as other members of the closely knit Mackle family, were frantic. The kidnappers had contacted Robert and demanded $500,000 in small bills, which he was to place in a suitcase and leave at a designated location on Biscayne Bay. Robert did as instructed shortly before dawn on the 19th.

When Mackle had left, the kidnappers glided silently in from the bay using a speedboat they had stolen from the University of Miami Institute of Marine Sciences. But they had hardly picked up the suitcase when they were spotted by two police officers, who, by the greatest coincidence, happened to be sitting in a car nearby. When the officers challenged the suspicious appearing pair, they dropped the suitcase and fled, one of them dashing through the yard of Herb Savage, architect of Marco's major buildings.

Both kidnappers escaped and contacted Robert once more the following day. This time the ransom was passed without incident. Yet the Mackles received no information about the whereabouts of their daughter.

It was then that the FBI issued warrants for the arrest of Gary Krist, an escaped convict from California who posed as a researcher at the Miami Institute, and Ruth Schier, a petite, Honduras-born biology researcher at the Institute. The theft of the speedboat had led the FBI to the pair. Krist was found hiding on a small island in Biscayne Bay.

Barbara was rescued late in the afternoon of the 20th. An amazing woman, she was in good spirits and said the kidnappers had actually treated her with a certain amount of consideration, given the situation. Her greatest concern during the ordeal was that her family was worrying about her. Later, at least partially at the urging of family friend, president-elect Richard Nixon, Barbara wrote of her experience in a book titled *83 Hours*.

But, while Barbara suffered no apparent effects of the ordeal, such was not the case with Robert Mackle, her father. "Frankly," Jim Vensel told me, "he never got over it."

Roberts Bay: Approval with String

Meanwhile the wearisome fight to secure the Roberts Bay dredge and fill permit continued. As 1969 dragged on with no Corps approval, Deltona realized it must obtain at least some of the fill from inland sites on the island. Accordingly, the location allotted to a church and a park at the block bounded by Winterberry, Peacock, Auburndale, and Barcelona became a large borrow pit 30 feet deep. However this was not enough and, as the company began to fall behind the schedule promised in the Coordinated Growth Plan, the purchasers began to grumble and the first talk was heard of lawsuits.

But all was not lost. The Mackle family had many pipelines to Washington and through them they learned that the Army Corps was not happy with the way the Department of the Interior was pushing into Corps territory. The Corps believed that the Interior was being far too hard on Deltona. In July 1969 Brigadier General F. P. Koisch, director of the Corps' Civil Works division, wrote to Interior's Under Secretary Russell Train that he viewed Deltona's dredge and fill request favorably. This feeling was

The Landmark Swamp, December 1967.

S.R. 92 is at the left, which is north. The Gulf of Mexico is on the bottom. Roberts Bay at the right top. Smokehouse Creek is in the center outlined partially by a mosquito dike. The dike also extends along the upper shore of Roberts Bay. Smokehouse was very shallow with many locations barely a foot or less above low tide. Almost the entire area in the center of the photo is swamp.

Clogging the Smokehouse Creek's mouth are Amelia Key and a portion of Maynard Key . The levels of both will be raised and serve as sites for some of Marco's most luxurious homes along South Heathwood and Caxambas Court.

Deltona's first airstrip cuts a wide swath down the photo's center. Running south from the airstrip is the narrow road which the Air Force laid to reach the missile tracking station at the photo's bottom right, now Deltona's construction headquarters.

Crescent Beach is almost entirely deserted except for the Voyager, then called the Marco Beach Hotel. Collier Boulevard ends at the hotel.

At the top left S.R. 953 crosses S.R. 92. Deltona's Sales and Administration building is at the junction. S.R. 953 continues south over a route no longer in existence to reach Caxambas Pass.

due to Deltona's cooperation in reducing the amount of material to be dredged, the company's promise to preserve a small mangrove island named John Key at the entry to Smokehouse Creek, and its agreement to erect a 10-acre island for environmental research in the midst of Roberts Bay.

Furthermore, General Koisch wrote, not only had approval been given by the State of Florida and the Collier

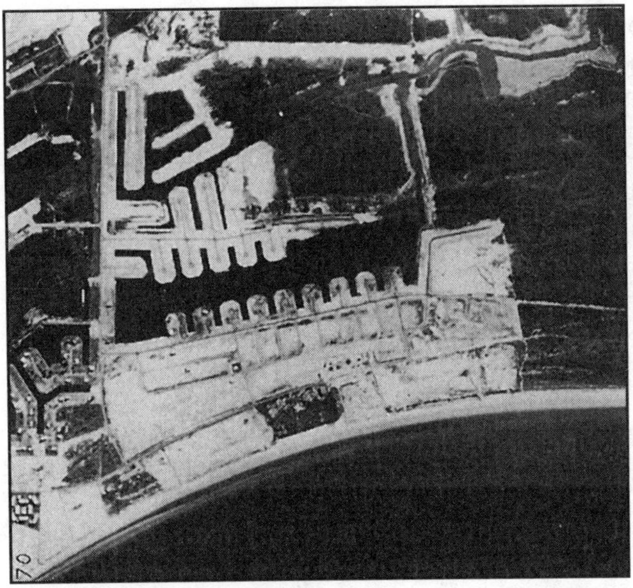

The Landmark Swamp, December 1970.

Much of the swamp has been converted to homesites and clear waterways. A large portion of the work was done by the dredge brought into the swamp from the north by way of a cut through S.R. 92. The refilled road cut can still be seen.

The former landing strip has now become Landmark Street, which connects with nine landthumbs including Maple, Spruce, and Ironwood.

Across the waterway Lamplighter drive takes shape, with Coronado, Dill and Dana Courts already laid out and Cara and Bond still being formed. Farther toward the top Shenandoah has emerged from the swamp but Whiteheart and Sunflower are still in the early stages.

Heathwood is being formed along the upper portion of the photo. The box-like piece of land above Heathwood is the edge of the Griffis-Vogstad parcel which will become the Frank Mackle Park. The Collier County Public Library will be built near Deltona's Sales and Administration Headquarters is at the extreme upper left on a triangle now occupied by a fire station. Meanwhile along the Gulf, the Voyager, with its bright pitch and putt golf course, stands out. Next to the Voyager, the first tower of the Marco Beach Hotel (now the Marriott) is being constructed.

County commissioners but by the Federal Water Pollution Control Administration as well. In addition, the dredging would actually improve navigation, which was a long-standing Corps goal.

It was for these reasons, Kiosch told Train, that he was going to recommend permit approval to the secretary of the Army, who was the final authority.

At long last, on December 8, 1969, more than two years after the request was submitted, Deltona received official notice from the Department of the Army that the Roberts Bay permit had been approved. There was great rejoicing at company headquarters as orders went out that the dredges and draglines could once more begin work.

But at the end of the letter was a sentence that tempered the good feeling. "The granting of this permit," the Army Department warned, "does not necessarily mean that future applications for work in the same area will be similarly granted." Of the five permit areas that Deltona had divided Marco into, the company had received approval for only two. There were even bigger fights to come.

7

Big Happenings, 1970-74

Although the fight for the Roberts Bay dredge and fill permit weighed heavily on the minds of Deltona executives, many other essential activities demanded their attention.

For one, there was the matter of a new chairman of the board of directors. Elliott Mackle resigned for health reasons early in 1970. The transition was not major, for Robert Mackle succeeded him and Jim Vensel took Robert's old seat on the board. Frank Mackle remained as president.

More pressing was the need to supplement the Voyager (then known as the Marco Beach Hotel), whose 100 rooms and forty-four villa units would soon be inadequate for the ever-increasing flood of tourists and Air Caravan guests coming to Marco.

The Mackles' first thought was to put up a square tower immediately south of the current units. They planned to install a restaurant on the summit offering a magnificent view of the Gulf and the marvelous Marco sunsets. But, under proddings of the finance and sales departments, they reluctantly concluded that a single story convention center would be both cheaper and more useful. So it was built instead, leaving Marco's sky-top restaurant a dream for the future.

Deltona officials plan the Marco Beach Hotel, 1968.

Frank Mackle leans over a scale model of the yet unbuilt Marco Beach Hotel, while an artist's sketch lies on the table. These are Deltona's top officials: (left to right) William O'Dowd (finances), James Vensel (architecture and engineering), Frank Mackle (president and CEO), Neil Bahr (sales), Elliott Mackle (executive vice president), Robert Mackle (secretary-treasurer), and Robert Whalen (hotel operations).

Planning the Marco Beach Hotel

Early in 1968, the Mackle brothers began considering an entirely new hotel. They wanted it to be a magnificent structure that they could promote as the keynote for the paradise they were creating at Marco. "We felt that the new hotel would make the island," Frank Mackle told me.

The brothers got designs from several architectural firms, but none satisfied them. Finally Frank approached Herbert Savage, Deltona's chief architect. He insisted Savage design the hotel himself and go to Hawaii to get the inspiration.

So Herb and his wife speeded off to the Pacific. Emily Savage dreamed of lazy days enjoying the beaches. But Herb had them booked at a breakneck pace. His wife asked him: "Can we relax and enjoy the trip?" "But I wouldn't hear of it," Herb reminisced. "I was running around everywhere taking pictures and making notes. That's all I thought of."

Inspired by Hawaii, Savage drew up plans for an eye-catching hotel. Greeting the guests on the grounds outside the entryway was a fountain, lily pond, and gushing waterfall, just as he had seen so often in Hawaii.

As for the lobby, it was very Polynesian, with its steeply pitched ceiling and wood beams capped with stylized Hawaiian bird head carvings. The impressive light fixtures were uniquely South Seas.

But the Mackles, too, put their imprint on the lobby. Frank Mackle, in particular, "insisted," Savage recalled, "that when a family entered the hotel, mom and the kids could see what dad was paying for." He wanted to give them an expansive view, not only of the spacious and luxurious interior, but of the pool and the blue Gulf beyond. "For this reason," Savage explained, "we raised the hotel's front entry and put a huge, two-story picture window at the far end of the lobby facing the water. We also imported very tall, bent palms from Miami to frame the window." Experienced travelers commented that they had seen no more impressive hotel entrance anywhere in the world.

On the north side, Savage designed a 10-story rectangular tower with bright mosaics gracing the frontal walls. The arching balcony railings were shaped like a similar handrail he had seen in Hawaii. But he made them larger than necessary to give an added proportion to the tower's grace.

On the south side Savage put a wing of two-story lanais set back from the pool area. Frank Mackle, especially, was pleased with the concept, and whenever he stayed at the hotel it was always in a lanai on the upper floor overlooking the beach.

At the Gulf end of the lanai wing, Savage placed Quinn's Restaurant and Lounge. It was based on a picturesque World War II bar Savage knew of on Tahiti.

Building the Jewel of the Gulf

The Mackles were eager to begin construction and even included a sketch of the proposed hotel in their annual

The Marco Beach Hotel being built in 1971.

The residents' beach is in the foreground, and between it and the hotel are the two story wings and villas of the Voyager Hotel.

report for 1968. They proclaimed that it would be not only the finest such structure on the entire Gulf of Mexico but a premier hotel in all of North America. However the financial department warned that the time was premature for such an expense, so it was not until 1970, when a $12 million loan was negotiated, that work could begin.

Savage's original plans provided the framework for the hotel as it went up. But some of his ideas were scrapped. One was his beloved Hawaiian waterfall, which had to be eliminated when the water pumps encountered trouble filtering the debris from the lilies and goldfish. Also dropped were the gaslights he originally installed around the pool and patio areas. He intended to hire Seminole Indians to canoe in from the Gulf each sunset carrying torches with which they would illuminate the gaslights. It was a colorful ceremony he had enjoyed in Hawaii. But the hotel manager warned that after the first three weeks there would be just two people carrying the torches: he and Savage. So the gaslights became electric.

Yet there were not many things that Savage was denied. He was almost always poking here and there as construction went on. "I stomped around so much," he told me, "that people would finally say OK, OK." Thus, when furniture was delivered that did not fit his specifications, he sent it all back, then flew to Detroit to show the manufacturer what he wanted. When the interior decorator, a flamboyant Englishman who drove around in a Rolls Royce, began pushing a certain wood paneling that he insisted was all the rage in the Bahamas, Savage booked the hotel manager and himself on a plane for Nassau to see for themselves. "It was a cheap yellow and we rejected it on the spot," Savage said. "I told them to make it the color of driftwood, and that's what it became. I usually had my way."

The tower rose before anything else. Savage insisted that the mosaic inlaid designs depict the history of the Mackles in Florida. "The Mackles were not enthused," Savage admitted, "for they were humble people." But, of course, the mosaics went in as Savage planned, with decorative pictures of sailboats, birds, saw grass, etc.

The artistic work was done by Chuck Dodson, a friend of Savage's from his days at the University of Illinois. "Dodson, along with his son and 15-year-old daughter, worked on the mosaics all summer," Savage recalled. "They used the parking lot across the street, which is now the tennis courts. Each morning they were all there. Dodson drew the pattern on a table. Then he and his kids would lay out the wire forms and masons would pour the cement. The panels were three-feet-by-three-feet wide and two inches thick."

Savage's basic design was followed almost as he originally conceived it. About the only modification was around the swimming pool, where the statue of a winsome mermaid named Margo was brought over from its original resting point on the grounds of the Voyager between the pitch and putt course and the beach. It had been cast in honor of local celebrity and early feminist, Dale Messick, creator of the popular comic strip, *Brenda Starr*, who had to change her first name from Dalia before she was taken seriously by publishers.

As work went on, it became clear that the hotel was exceeding the cost estimates. "We got three-fourths of the way through the construction and I notified the Mackles that we needed more money," Savage told me. "So they went out and borrowed $2 million more. They didn't quibble. They wanted the best."

The only major mistake was the floor, a blue-black ceramic product which was so rough that the luggage carts bounced all over and made a racket. Ultimately balloon tires had to be installed on the carts. Savage had objected to the floor from the beginning, so he was not surprised when Marriott later ripped it out and installed smooth marble tile from Italy.

The Hotel's Grand Opening

The hotel opened in December 1971 to a gala ceremony attended by many dignitaries including Florida's governor, Reubin Askew. The distinguished guests met in the lobby glittering with colorful decorations. After a speech by the governor, Frank and Robert Mackle tugged on a pair of bows that held a bright, floor- to-ceiling paper partition which sealed off the lobby from the hall leading to the convention wing. As music played, the paper fell and the Mackles, along with Gov. Askew, Archbishop Coleman Carroll, and Neil Bahr, Deltona's chief operating officer, marched through the opening.

It was a moment no one there would ever forget. For Frank Mackle it was particularly significant, since it was he who had pushed the hardest for the sumptuous hotel. Later he proudly glowed to his shareholders that the hotel, with

The Marco Beach Hotel in 1972.

The hotel has just been opened. The plantings are so new that the palms still have their supports. Notice the waterfall and the Hawaiian-style pond. The waterfall was turned off and the pond filled in when filtration problems became too great.

its 370 luxurious units and multitude of meeting rooms, ranks as the largest, most complete resort and convention facility on Florida's West Coast." It was Deltona's finest moment.

The High-Rise Quintet

At the same time, Deltona was moving ahead in other areas. The company had chosen an area a half-mile or so up Crescent Beach as the location for its high-rise condos. The dazzling, seven-story Emerald Beach had been the first to go up in 1965, and two years later the Sunset House, with a unique 'Y' design, had followed. Then, in 1970, even while the Marco Beach Hotel was being built, Deltona constructed a second Y-shaped condo called Sunset House, North,

Deltona's high rises, 1971.

The Tradewinds is under construction. Its odd angle to the beach was caused when architects from an outside firm designed it larger than the lot was zoned for!

The Emerald Beach condominium is to the left of the Tradewinds. It was built in 1965 and was Deltona's original showplace condo. Notice the setbacks, which permit six of the eight units on each floor to have views of the Gulf.

The next building on the left is the Sunset House. Its Y-shape was also designed to permit maximum Gulf vistas. This design was repeated with its sister building, the Sunset House, North, which stands beside it.

Deltona also put up the Sea Breeze low rises between Seaview Court and Collier Boulevard, at the extreme upper right of the photo.

The body of water at the upper portion of the photo is Clam Bay.

beside its sister. The names of the twin condos reflected the beautiful sunsets for which Marco was becoming famous. Almost simultaneously plans were laid out for the fourth high rise of the group, to be named the Tradewinds.

Deltona had an unusual experience with the Tradewinds. Since the company's own architectural department was too busy to handle it, they gave the design assignment to an outside firm. After the detailed blueprints had been drawn, it was found that the building was slightly too large for the lot! Rather than spend the relatively large sum to redesign the building, Deltona simply turned it to a slight angle so it would fit the lot.

The Tradewinds, with its flamboyant roofs, was astonishingly expensive. At 12 stories, it was the tallest building on the island. Yet it was a tremendous success when it opened in 1972. None other than James Vensel, Deltona's master architect who laid out the entire island and named its streets, purchased a unit in the building which he kept for many years.

Meanwhile, two even grander high-rise buildings were on Deltona's drawing boards: the Admiralty House, which would be 17 stories; and, the lofty Gulfview, which would cut the clouds with 21 stories. At the same time, across Collier Boulevard, work was being done on the Island Manor, a 169 unit, two- and three-story complex.

Deltona Expands Into Many Fields

The early 1970s were heady days at Deltona. The dredge permit matter with the Army Corps of Engineers, while aggravating, was not seen as particularly threatening. Indeed, Frank Mackle received a reassuring legal opinion from his attorney that a Corps denial of Deltona's request would amount to the taking of the company's property without compensation. That, of course, was prohibited by the Constitution.

It was not only at Marco that the company was moving ahead. Deltona was also developing seven other communities in Florida. Within these communities Deltona usually owned, not only the lots, but the shopping center, a hotel, and the utility company. In one community, Deltona even owned a nearby radio station.

In addition, Deltona was branching into related businesses. In 1968 it bought the Imperial Lumber Co., which retailed wood products to large contractors throughout Florida. In the same year it purchased Fortune Homes, producer of mobile homes. A while later it formed its own realty companies to handle property resales at Marco and other locations; and shortly thereafter organized the Deltona Mortgage Co. to provide financing for these sales. Later Deltona's Florida Interiors company began to sell home furnishings.

At Marco, Deltona's Neil Bahr was instrumental in founding the First Bank of Marco, now part of the NationsBank system, in which it owned a significant portion of the stock. Herb Savage designed the bank building, which until 1998 stood on the southeast corner of Collier Boulevard and Bald Eagle. When First Bank constructed a second building on Barfield Drive beside Deltona's Administration Headquarters, Savage designed that, too.

Deltona's Airline

In 1972 the company formed the Marco Island Airways, with three, 15-passenger Beechcraft flying five round trips daily between Marco and Miami, where they linked up with major passenger lines connecting with every important northern city. The planes were white, with a green and a blue line running along their bodies symbolizing palms and water. At Marco the planes landed at an impressive 4,000 foot airstrip that ran along what would become Edgewater and Bonita Courts. There was a four-room terminal at Bonita from which a road crossed the future Cottonwood Court to connect with S.R. 92.

To handle all this activity Deltona engaged in a whirlwind of hiring. By the end of 1972 the number of employees shot up to 4,100, a 40 percent gain in just two years. The architecture and building design department alone had 100 persons.

Deltona's executives receive an award, 1972.

Holding Deltona's award from the City of Miami for the architectural merit of its headquarters at 3250 S. W. Third Avenue are Frank Mackle on the left and Robert Mackle on the right. Also in the foreground, James Vensel stands beside Frank and Neil Bahr beside Robert. Herbert Savage, with eyeglasses, stands immediately behind the award. The others are part of Deltona's architectural department.

And to house the expansion Deltona constructed a six story addition to its original three-story home office in Miami, for which it won an architectural award.

Building the Luxurious Estates Area

Despite Deltona's success in many diverse fields, the sale of lots and homes remained the company's main field of endeavor, providing 85 percent of total revenues.

In the beginning the Mackles had assumed that buyers would be interested in modest, easily affordable homes, many of them vacation residences. For this reason, the early lots on the northeast portion of the island were small and the homes relatively inexpensive, with most containing garages that accommodated only a single car.

But Deltona quickly learned that many persons were willing to spend considerable sums to own a home on this sub-tropical paradise. For this reason the company set aside a portion of the Roberts Bay permit zone for larger properties. It was called the Estates Area.

The Estates was bordered by Smokehouse Creek on the west, Barfield Bay on the east, and Winterberry Drive on the north. Originally Deltona planned to run a wall between Winterberry and Collingswood to give the Estates a formal boundary. Although the wall was never built, due to Deltona's later financial difficulties, a green belt where the wall would have been still remains between the two streets.

What was to become the Estates area was pretty well isolated from the rest of the island. The road, the southern portion of which later became Barfield Drive, was sand and shells, including some sharp conchs the size of rocks. "If you made it [down the road] three times without a puncture," recalled Deputy Sheriff Les Binns, Marco's lone law enforcement officer at this time, "you had a good day."

Deltona owned most, but not quite all, of the land around Roberts Bay. A plot was left to Lawrence Pettit. Pettit, an enterprising man, turned his living room into a tavern, which the construction men liked to frequent. Soon the place acquired notoriety as the "Bucket of Blood." "It lived up to its name," was Officer Binns' comment. Binns wisely made friends with some of the toughest workers, for his only way to summon reinforcements from Naples was by means of his car radio, which often did not work until he drove to the top of Indian Hill. Even then, it would take 20 minutes, with sirens shrieking, for a sheriff's car to reach Marco.

In addition to the Bucket of Blood, Pettit also built some shanties nearby, which he called the Ideal Fish Camp. The disreputable shacks, sometimes frequented by drug dealers and smugglers, besmirched the area that would become Osceola Court for many years – even after Deltona's luxurious homes began dotting the area. It was not until 1989 that the county received authority to condemn the disreputable place. Then, at long last, it was put to the torch.

In 1970, immediately after receiving the Roberts Bay dredge and fill permit, Deltona started development in earnest. Work was resumed on Fredrick Bay, and on Hammock, Conover, and Alameda Courts, all of which had been halted by Corps order for 15 agonizing months! By the end of 1971 Roberts Bay had been defined by seawalls, and Ludlow Drive had been laid amid the uplands of the bay's southern portion.

During 1971 and 1972 Deltona kept up the pace. A short causeway was built across Smokehouse Creek from Mimosa to Forrest Court, thereby enabling machinery from construction headquarters at the old Air Force Missile Tracking Station on Cape Marco to gain more easy access to Amelia Key. Soon the water separating the key from the main part of the island to the north was filled in.

About this time a second causeway was built across Smokehouse Creek from the future public marine facility to Maynard Key. The key had been named for the first sheriff of Collier County, W R. Maynard, who had been a hotshot pilot during World War 1, and in 1928 had soared over Collier County filming the first detailed aerial survey.

After Maynard Key was elevated with fill from Roberts Bay, Caxambas Court was constructed across the key and connected by means of a small bridge with Barfield Drive to the east. Then the temporary causeway across Smokehouse Creek was removed.

The year 1972 was also the year when Copeland Drive was constructed. Here Deltona's master architect, Vensel, honored David Graham Copeland. Copeland had been a prominent figure in Collier County from his colorful beginnings as head of the Southwest Florida Mounted Police to his position as long time general manager for the Barron Collier companies.

Roberts Bay looking north in 1971.

Roberts Bay is in the lower center of the photo, with Barfield Bay on the extreme right and the Gulf of Mexico on the extreme left. Completed on Roberts Bay are the land fingers which will become Hammock, Conover, Alameda and Sandhill. The stubbly thumb of Devon Court protrudes into the eastern portion of the bay. Much of Ludlow Road has been formed at the bottom right.

Mosquito dikes in the left foreground outline comma-shaped Amelia Key and Maynard Key beneath it. On Amelia Key the first work is being done on Forrest Street, which will soon extend across the thin channel that separates the key from the island proper. The Caxambas Court bridge, which will connect Maynard key with the main island, will not be built for two more years.

Work has just started on the area of the public boat ramp at the extreme lower left. A temporary bridge will soon connect it with Maynard Key at this Point.

Dark patches along Crescent Beach to the left are occupied by the Voyager Hotel and the brand new Marco Beach Hotel which will be proudly opened at the end of the year. The paved portion of Collier Boulevard ends just south of the Marco Beach Hotel. The street continues unpaved only as far as what will be Winterberry.

S.R. 92 cuts across the upper middle of the photo from east to west. Above it, at the left center, Deltona's second temporary airstrip can be seen in the Unit Six swamp. The golf course is above S.R. 92 on the right portion of the photo. The S.R. 951 bridge to the mainland reaches over the Marco River in the upper right.

Land Sales Halted, 1973

By the end of 1973, work in the two areas where Deltona had dredging permits was largely completed. Thus along the Marco River Area and Roberts Bay the waterways had been dug, the seawalls installed, and the land raised. Homes could now be built. The company had performed its obligations under the sales contracts.

But contracts had also been sold for Marco's remaining three areas for which permits had not yet been granted. These were Collier Bay, Barfield Bay, and Big Key, just north of the road to Goodland. Work could not begin here until the Army Corps of Engineers granted dredging permits. Deltona had begun selling land contracts in these areas back in 1965, when the island was first opened. At this time there was no question but what the company had a perfect right to do so. Although in June of 1973 all land sales in the areas without permits stopped, by this time Collier Bay was three-fourths sold, Barfield 90 percent sold, and Big Key nearly 100 percent! Thus it was far too late to protect Deltona from severe repercussions if the permits were denied for any of these three areas.

Yet as the year ended the Mackle brothers tried to be optimistic. "Despite the temporary obstacles that we faced...," Frank told his stockholders, "Your management believes that the future is shaping up as one of great opportunity...We anticipate a strong performance in 1974."

It was not to be.

8

The Climactic Battle, 1975

By 1974 the days of reckoning that Deltona had dreaded for so long descended on the company. Forewarnings had been sounding for many years. There had been the long proceedings in the late 1960s involved with the permit to develop the Roberts Bay area. Then in 1971 the Army Corps of Engineers had issued a surprise cease and desist order for work inland from Collier Bay, indicating for the first time that it would exert jurisdiction over interior wetlands in addition to exterior, navigable waterways. Two years later Deltona had been forced to stop all land sales in Marco's remaining undeveloped permit areas. Meanwhile, the dredging permit requests for Collier Bay, Barfield Bay and the waters around Big Key kept dragging on.

The Kice Island Giveaway

Deltona had grave apprehensions about the Roberts Bay permit negotiations. The company realized that it must have as many allies as possible. One of these could be the State of Florida's powerful Trustees of the Internal Improvement Fund (TIIF). Toward the end of 1971 Deltona signed an agreement whereby the TIIF would issue a renewal permit for Roberts Bay and also help the company present its

Aerial photo of Marco, 1975

Deltona has almost completed the island's lower Portion. S.R. 92 enters the photo at the lower left and continues to the Gulf of Mexico in the distance. Crescent Beach south of S.R. 92 still has only one high rise: the Marco Beach Hotel (now the Marriott).

John Steven's Creek is in the center foreground, bordered by Stillwater Court. To the right Polynesia Court, with a sprinkling of homes, fronts the Marco River stem streets, Honduras and Barbados, connect with Barfield Drive, which makes a soft U across the lower middle of the photo. The dark area above Barfield to the right is the golf course, bordered by Nassau and Jamaica Courts.

case before the Federal Corps for which, in return, Deltona would cede to the state Kice Island and other lands totaling 4,000 acres.

The loss of Kice Island, bordering Marco on the south, was no little matter. Deltona had seen the island as an important addition to the Marco complex, for its shore was every bit as lovely as Marco's Crescent Beach. Deltona planned to connect Kice to Marco by way of a series of scenic bridges and a roadway wending through Horr's Island to link with S.R. 92, a short distance west of Goodland.

Mounting Problems Caused by the Permit Delay

Deltona experienced a steep decline in Marco's land and home sales in 1974. Further diminution in revenues resulted from individuals refusing to pay on contracts they had made for lots that Deltona could not deliver because of the delay in the Army Corps dredge and fill permits. To make matters worse, a national recession occurred at this time resulting in an operating loss at the Marco Beach Hotel due to decreased occupancy. The recession also caused fewer sales at Deltona's seven other smaller communities across Florida. A loss, too, was experienced by Deltona's lumber division because of lower construction activity throughout Florida.

While revenues diminished, expenses rose. A large proportion of these expenses consisted of interest payments on bank loans tied to the prime rate that was soaring toward 12 percent.

The result was a net loss of nearly $7 million for the year. Company officials were severely shaken.

News of Deltona's problems had a catastrophic effect on the company's stock. In 1970 prices had climbed to an all-time peak of $70 per share. Deltona employees who had purchased stock in 1963 at $12 had become wealthy persons. But by the end of 1974 the stock had plunged to a low of just $3! This was a major calamity to many stockholders.

The Banks Force Deltona to Sell Assets

Now the banks who had loaned Deltona large sums became concerned. They demanded that Deltona obtain revenue from other sources – namely the selling of its assets.

This was exceedingly distasteful to Deltona, since it meant that the company would turn from a dynamic,

Deltona's high command around 1972.

At this time Frank Mackle (on the left) was Deltona's president and Robert Mackle (in the center) was chairman of the board. Neil Bahr (on the right) was executive vice president, Deltona's number three man. It was he who arranged the heart-wrenching sale of the hotel to Marriott in 1979.

expanding entity into a contracting one. Yet there was no choice. They must have money to meet their bills. Accordingly, late in 1974, Bahr, number three man behind the two Mackles, was relieved of his position as chief operating officer and told to form a subsidiary to handle the painful downsizing.

For this purpose, Bahr formed the Deltona Land and Investment Corp. late in 1974. Shortly thereafter he moved out of the Deltona Building in Miami and located in Coral Gables so as to remove himself from the turmoil at headquarters. Nonetheless, the upsetting feeling followed him. "I was not happy about doing the selling," Bahr remembered. "The whole complexion of the company changed. It was something we had never anticipated: that we would be setting up a corporation to dispose of assets to keep the parent alive. Work had been fun up to that time. It wasn't any longer."

By this time it was apparent that the company's future, perhaps its very existence, depended on obtaining the dredge and fill permits from the Army Corps for the remaining three areas: Collier Bay, Barfield Bay, and Big Key.

As 1975 dawned, the Corps announced it would hold hearings on Deltona's permit applications, which had been submitted two long years earlier. Deltona knew this would be a crucial event. Company officials, headed by Vensel, and a battery of lawyers and engineering experts began preparing.

So did Deltona's opponents.

Enter the Conservancy

Deltona's problems with the Army Corps were compounded greatly by a local environmental group called the Conservancy. The Conservancy was started several years earlier when some wealthy retirees gathered at the Naples home of Lester Norris to discuss opposing a planned highway from Naples to Rookery Bay, a few miles north of Marco. The group got more than 1000 persons to sign an anti-highway petition and forced the Collier County commissioners to veto the proposal.

Thrilled by its success, yet concerned that other developers might want to put homes and hotels on the Rookery Bay islands, the group decided to purchase the entire area and turn it into a preserve. It now formally organized itself into the Collier County Conservancy, an adjunct of the Nature Conservancy, a national organization. Again the group effectively mobilized the public – this time mustering 1400 individual donations to the Rookery Bay fund.

On April 19, 1966 the Conservancy presented title for 1600 acres at Rookery Bay to the National Audubon Society to manage as a nature sanctuary. Within a few years the preserve had swelled to 4,000 acres and bordered a wilderness to the south owned by a branch of the Barron Collier family. The Collier-Read tract, as it was called, consisted of 9,000 acres. It was a natural buffer between the Rookery Bay sanctuary and Deltona's Marco Island development immediately south.

At this time the Conservancy, with Willard Merrihue at the helm, viewed Deltona's activities on Marco as unfortunate, but nothing about which the group should become involved. This feeling changed in 1969 when Deltona bought the Collier-Read tract, incorporated it into its Marco Shores division, and made plans to develop a portion of it into a Venetian-style village.

Vensel drew up the streets and zoned the locations for a shopping center, parks, schools, churches, and homesites on an intricate system of waterways. Approvals were obtained from the county and state, and a rough road connecting with S.R. 951 just above Mainsail Drive was laid westward through the swamp for prospective buyers to view the location. Sales boomed and quickly over 3700 homesites were contracted for.

The Conservancy's attack on Deltona was headed by Bernie Yokel, a young former football player from Ohio. Yokel had come to the Conservancy by way of the University of Miami's Institute of Marine Science, from which he had a master's degree in fisheries and was working on a Ph.D. in estuarine ecology.

Yokel had always been fascinated by water and the creatures who inhabited it. "All my available spare time I spend on or under the water," he told me. I got wrapped up in marine biology and Cousteau's *Silent World*. I gobbled up water articles as fast as they were published."

In 1970 Yokel, with his wife and four children, moved into a scenic home which the Conservancy had just purchased

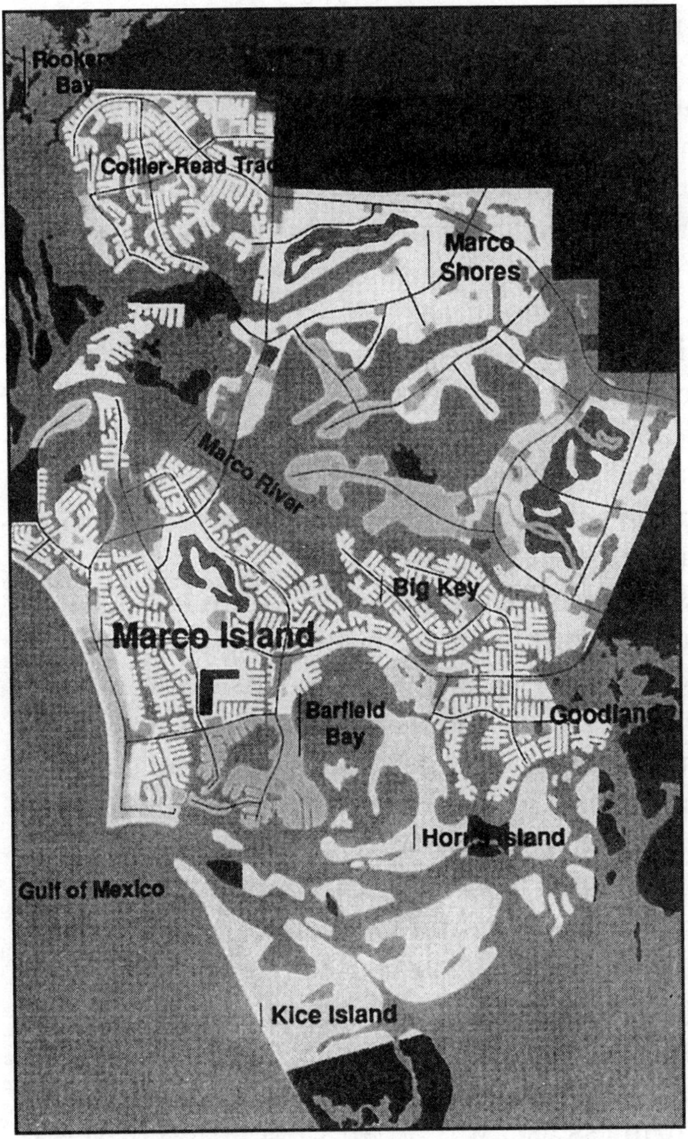

Deltona's ultimate plans for development.

This map appeared in Deltona's annual report for 1970. It shows the company's overall layout for the nearly 20,000 acres of the island and surrounding shores.

Only a fraction of this was actually developed. Deltona had well-advanced plans for Barfield Bay, Big Key and the Collier-Read Tract. These plans were ended by actions at the Army Corps of Engineers. Marco Shores, too, was greatly restricted and ultimately large sections were sold to help pay bank creditors. Kice Island with its luscious beach became a state sanctuary. Development of portions of Horr's Island was permitted, but by the time Deltona was ready for it in the late 1980s the company lacked the funds and was forced to sell the island.

as a research center in Rookery Bay. Yokel, intense and extroverted, was a born activist. He quickly joined a host of committees in Collier County – and was soon a sort of public hero, so noted the Conservancy Yearbook.

Yokel regarded Deltona's plans for the Collier-Read Tract as a "gauntlet which had been dropped." He was convinced that once the dredge and fill operation began, Rookery Bay was bound to become polluted.

Yokel, acting with Joel Kuperberg, the Conservancy's executive director, sent a letter to the Florida Department of Pollution Control complaining of Deltona's activities. It struck a responsive chord and they were rewarded a series of hearings. Soon other agencies were contacted and more hearings resulted.

These constant hearings put a severe strain on Deltona. Yokel was quite candid to me about using such tactics: "Compared with today they might be considered unethical. But in early 1970 you had no Clean Water Act or EPA [Environmental Protection Agency]. All you could do was to ask for hearings and seek to delay the project. Since that was our only tool, that was what we used."

The delaying tactics paid off. At the end of 1970 Congress passed the Environmental Protection Act, which set up the EPA, a watch dog with teeth. Then in 1972, the monumental Clean Water Act came into force. A year later the Endangered Species Act became law.

Less dramatic than the national acts, but even more pertinent to Deltona's case, was a pair of doctoral dissertations which appeared at this time. Written by Eric Heald and William Odom, they showed that mangroves were a basic energy source in the complex web of life that existed along the south Florida Gulf coast. The wish-wash of tidal nutrients through the mangroves' tangled roots was like a cradle nurturing uncountable creatures that enriched the ocean. "In a matter of just two or three years," Yokel said, "the mangrove became a sort of sacred tree. It was vital to the fish, shrimp, crabs and all the exciting things that come out of the bays: those things we wanted to save. 'Thou shalt not destroy red mangroves' was our call to arms."

When, in 1975, the Army Corps announced that it had scheduled a final hearing on Sept. 2 and 3 relative to the Collier Bay, Barfield Bay, and Big Key permits, Yokel and his friends began making plans. This would be the climactic battle in the war which had been running for five years. They would be ready!

Epic Changes at the Army Corps of Engineers

The Army Corps of Engineers was not the same organization it had been in prior years. By means of the Water Pollution Control Act Amendments of 1972, Congress had delegated to the Corps authority over wetlands, small streams, and even freshwater swamps. The Corps, used to dealing with deep waterways, was reluctant to move into its new sphere. So the National Wildlife Federation and the Natural Resources Defense Council sued the agency, and in the spring of 1975 a federal judge ruled that the Corps must accept its new responsibilities. Thus, when the hearings began barely a half-year later, the Corps was still reeling from its experience at court.

In order to pacify its environmental detractors, the Corps appointed Col. Donald Wisdom, district engineer, to head its hearing. Wisdom was a tough soldier who had served as an advisor in Vietnam. Known to describe himself as a "bad-ass"– so reported the *Smithsonian* magazine – he was one of the new breed that was attempting to drag the Corps into line with the current environmental thinking.

Deltona Prepares for the Crucial Hearings

Deltona assigned its case to Jack Peeples, attorney par excellence. Peeples was a most capable and learned lawyer. He had a fantastic memory and could not only present a case without using notes but spoke with a clarity and decisiveness that carried many a jury. "He was," Yokel remembered, "the silver tongue of Deltona and an extremely effective adversary."

Peeples had ample ammunition for the hearings due mainly to the efforts of Vensel, Deltona's long-time point man in dealing with the Corps and various environmental groups. Vensel and others had collected enough supporting documents to fill a bookshelf more than 6 feet long!

Peeples and the top Deltona executives held many meetings relative to the upcoming hearings. Each official was assigned a topic and rehearsed what he would say. Each knew his specialty intimately. There was no technical question for which someone at Deltona would not be ready with an incisive answer.

Deltona was confident. After all, the company already had approvals by every state and local agency with an interest in the project. Local sentiment was so overwhelmingly for permit approval that petitions carrying 11,900 signatures had been sent to the Corps – compared with 1,217 signatures on petitions against approval.

Also, Deltona felt that, when the final call was made, 'it could count on the Corps, for it was basically a kindred spirit– "they're engineers; our kind of people," Frank Mackle asserted.

The Environmentalists Mobilize

Meanwhile the environmentalists prepared their own strategy. The local Conservancy did not stand alone. The 40,000 member national Environmental Defense Fund had been set up for situations like this. The Fund provided the Conservancy with a very capable counsel, James Tripp. "He was," according to Yokel, "the best damned attorney at cross examinations I've ever seen. He'd leave you sitting in your own blood and you wouldn't even know you'd been cut."

Tripp came down to Rookery Bay shortly before the hearing. Some 19 separate environmental organizations across the nation joined with the Collier County Conservancy. These included the National Conservancy, the Sierra Club, and the Florida Audubon Society. Many sent experts in hydrology and estuarine ecology. Tripp coached and directed each witness so he would present his testimony most effectively. He coalesced the diverse group into a unified battering ram designed to pierce Deltona's rocky bulwarks.

The Army Corps Hearing Begins

The day came and everyone was ready. "Marco Battle Opens Today" headlined the *Naples Daily News*. Col. Wisdom would be conducting the hearing over two days, with the first session beginning at 1:30 p.m. on Tuesday. The site was at Lely High School, a new building that was part hurricane shelter, on the Naples' south side.

Lely was constructed like a rambling, two-story blockhouse. Its exterior was dull, off-white cement. There were few windows. Inside, the auditorium was shaped similar to an armory, with a high, arching ceiling and walls devoid of decorations. There was a wide stage at the far end where Col. Wisdom set up. With him were a pair of Corps officials: one, the permits chief and, the other, the director of the environmental division. Also on the stage was Jack Ravan from the powerful EPA in Atlanta.

The auditorium was jammed with more than a thousand partisans. Environmentalists were there, mostly from the Conservancy, but many from the other organizations supporting Yokel and Tripp, who would make the principal presentations. In their corner, too, were officials from the U.S. Fish and Wildlife Service as well as the National Marine Fisheries. They recognized that this was a precedent-setting hearing – the first where it would be decided if a private company had the right to develop wetlands that did not involve navigational waters without government restrictions.

Most of the persons at the meeting were for the development of Marco. A group from the Marco Island Civic Association said the permits should be given because most property owners bought their lots "on the basis the island development would be carried through to completion." And there was the president of the Marco Chamber of Commerce, who felt that the Corps had no right to deny the permits when local county and state authorities, who knew the area far better than the feds, had already given approval. They were supported by hundreds of residents.

Even more vocal than Marco's citizens were union construction workers. They rolled up in a cavalcade of buses, wearing their hard hats and carrying such signs as "Take the Shackles off the Mackles" and "Environmentalists Are Polluting Our Economy." During full construction they had 700 or more men on the site earning money for their families. Now their number was down to about 80 and they were incensed. Yokel thought that Deltona had imported them especially for intimidation, but company officials claimed the union was no friend of Deltona's, not with the strikes and conflicts that had sometimes plagued the project.

It may have been different with other company supporters. Yokel overheard some of them talking in the hall. They didn't know what they were doing at Lely; Deltona had picked them up at the Marco Beach Hotel and told them they were going on a free picnic!

Deltona States its Case

Deltona was given the opportunity to make its argument at the beginning. It emphasized five main points:

First, the company was not an irresponsible polluter, as its opponents claimed. Deltona had always worked with local and state officials in environmentally responsible ways. It had set Marco aside as an eagle sanctuary. It had closed off the waterways when it dredged to avoid contaminating the surrounding waters. It had put "diaper" nets around its dredging equipment when working in swampy areas. It had made a nature preserve of three islands in the Marco River. As a result of these and other actions, the Federal Fish and Wildlife Service had originally commended the company for its "farsighted recognition" of natural resources.

Second, Deltona had already sold most of the land in question. There were 4,900 homesites promised in the three areas where permits had not yet been granted. Most of the lot sales had occurred in the 1960s when there was every reason to expect that the dredge and fill permits for these areas would be granted with the ease of the first permit. Therefore it would be unfair to punish a company with violating a series of laws that had not been passed at the time of the alleged violation.

Third, Deltona's development of the land in question would not, as the Department of the Interior claimed, cause extensive damages to the ecology of the area. The mangroves in the three permit zones represented only a minuscule portion of Florida's mangroves. There were only 2,200 acres in question. This was a bare one-half of 1 percent of the state's mangroves!

Should one look out from the top either of the two high-rise bridges leading to Marco, as far as he could see would be mangroves. Indeed, they extended southward for nearly a hundred miles through the Everglades National Park, a 1.4 million acre preserve.

Actually the role of the red mangrove might not be as vital as the Heald and Odom dissertations made out. Deltona had used Heald as a consultant and his later work suggested that the mangroves were more important farther south in the Ten Thousand Islands than at Marco.

Fourth, Deltona had compensated for the destruction of Marco's mangrove breeding grounds by erecting a pair of artificial reefs a couple miles off the island. These reefs, each a mile long and a half-mile wide, consisted of compressed tires and other debris and were proving to be effective habitats for plants and sea creatures that could not exist on the Gulf's sandy, featureless bottom. Deltona's Applied Marine Ecology Station, with a dozen trained specialists, was supervising activities on the reefs and around Marco.

Deltona had no plans to expand its Marco project beyond the 6,700 acres it owned on Marco Island and the 12,800 acres on the mainland to the north and Horr's Island to the south. Indeed, Deltona's much promoted 'Coordinated Growth Program' emphasized that company communities would never exceed 20,000-25,000 acres.

Finally, Deltona asserted that denial of the permits would make it impossible for the company to develop the land and thus would make it worthless. This would amount to the taking of Deltona's possessions without compensation. Such an action was unconstitutional.

The Environmentalists Counterattack

The hearings resumed the following morning with Yokel, Tripp and other environmentalists making their case:

Although it was true, they said, that Deltona believed it was acting as an environmentally responsible company, the actions it had taken were only those that should have been forced on it. And although many conservationist groups had commended the company early on, that was before the movement really took shape in the early 1970s. By this time the pendulum had swung far beyond what Deltona was prepared to do to save the environment.

As for already having sold much of the land for which permits were now in question, that was the company's problem, not the environmentalists. From the very beginning Deltona was aware that development of the swampy sites involved obtaining government permits. The company should have put this stipulation into the contracts it made with the homesite purchasers. It was a regrettable fact that the initial permit came so easily that the company was lulled into believing the others would be the same. But uncertainties are part of economic reality and successful organizations must plan for unexpected future events.

Deltona made much of the fact that an exemption to its operations at Marco should be "grandfathered" into interpretation of the laws. However there was no legitimate reason for this, since the disputed permit areas were merely in the planning stage, not in active development.

The claim that the Marco area was so small that it had

almost no effect on the environment was irrelevant. The whole earth was composed of small areas and if you exempted one, then you should exempt another... and another... until everything would be exempted. The Marco decision would be precedent setting. Developers, as well as environmental groups, from around the nation were watching it. An example must be made of the company. The fact that Deltona was run by highly reputable individuals made it even more essential to deny the permits, since this would demonstrate that no one would be exempted.

And, finally, Deltona's point that refusing to let the company develop the permit areas would amount to taking its property without compensation. That was a matter for the courts to decide. It was not something that had any pertinence for this hearing.

And so the stormy session went on. Deltona countered the environmentalists' charges, decrying that the very existence of a noble company was being threatened over a few fish! It questioned whether an insignificant number of scrubby trees was worth wrecking the home plans of five thousand families? The union men sometimes rumbled so loudly that Col. Wisdom had to ask the speakers to shout into the microphones.

But at last it was over. The Corps' representatives packed up their papers and headed back to Washington. It would be up to the Defense Department higher-ups now. The decision would be made in a few months.

Until then there was nothing to do but wait.

9

THE FINAL GAMBLE, 1976-83

The headline of the *Miami Herald* for April 17, 1976 told it all: "Marco Island Projects Blocked." The Army Corps of Engineers had at last made its decision. Of the three dredge and fill permit applications which Deltona had submitted, Barfield Bay and Big Key were denied. Only the smallest of the trio, Collier Bay, was granted.

Deltona was dumfounded. Right up until the last moment company officials had believed "grandfathering," based on the laws in effect when Deltona had begun the Marco project, would ensure approval.

Frank Mackle commented to the press that he was "shocked and outraged at the injustice." Later he told his stockholders in utter disgust that "the development work in question had been approved by all other jurisdictions in a period of hearings and examinations that extended over four years." Furthermore, "The Corps had been advised of the proposed work in detail as long ago as 1964."

The Specter of Bankruptcy

Altogether nearly 4,000 homesteads in Big Key and Barfield Bay had been sold and could not now be delivered. This represented a sum of $45 million principal and interest

Marco Island in 1976.

This photo looks down upon the north end of Marco. Bald Eagle Drive (S.R. 953) runs southward through the center until it ends as a fork at S.R. 92 in the upper portion of the picture. The land between Bald Eagle, S.R. 92, and the Gulf comprised the Collier Bay Permit Area. Work would not be carried on here until Deltona received Corps' approval to dredge in 1976.

At the time the photo was taken Deltona was erecting fingers of Land that will form the Crescent and Tigertail Street groups. They cluster around Smokehouse Bay at the lower right. At the same time the Giralda group is being formed on the margin of Collier Bay at the corner right.

Meanwhile dredgings from Smokehouse Bay have raised the swampy land at Bald Eagle and Collier Boulevard in preparation for the construction of the Island Plaza Shopping Center on the northwest corner and, much later, the SunBank Centre on the northeast corner.

that had been paid the company and was now subject to refund.

And there were further ramifications. The Marco Island rejections meant that sales in the Collier-Read portion of Marco Shores were certain to be disapproved. This involved 3,700 more lots with a potential refund of $34 million principal and interest!

To meet this $79 million liability Deltona had $7 million in cash, $51 million in land held for future investment, and $42 million in commercial and residential buildings. But since most of the land and buildings were encumbered with mortgages, there was actually no way, under present circumstances, that the company could refund the money involved. The Mackles were advised to take bankruptcy.

Just the thought of it roused Frank Mackle's ire. "I never even contemplated bankruptcy!" Frank told me years later. "it would have wiped everybody out." He paused, then added more softly, "But Deltona would be a prosperous company now."

If not bankruptcy, then what?

Deltona Takes the Offensive on Three Fronts

The Mackles decided to meet the difficulties head on. First, they would call on the courts to overturn what they were convinced was an unfair and arbitrary ruling by the Army Corps. Second, they would try to convince most contract holders to take their compensation in the form of other land from Deltona's vast holdings rather than cash. And, third, they would regenerate their profits by launching a massive building program the likes of which Florida had seldom seen!

Deltona Wins Its Initial Lawsuit Against the Army Corps

Almost as soon as the Corps rejected Deltona's permit request, the company began its lawsuits. There were two separate court cases. One asserted, as Deltona had contended all along, that the Corps' whole procedure was unconstitutional and should be set aside. The other that, should the permit denial not be voided, Deltona should receive money for the loss it suffered when the government took away the use of its land without compensation.

Late in 1980 there was great rejoicing at Deltona as the U.S. Court of Claims ruled that the denial of the dredge and fill permits had, indeed, resulted in the taking of Deltona's land by the doctrine of "inverse condemnation." The judgement was that unless the Corps reversed its decision, Deltona should receive compensation for the Corps' unlawful act.

Although the exact amount of the compensation was not yet determined and although the defendants appealed the case, the outcome looked good for the company at this point.

The Crucial Matter of Refunds

Meanwhile Deltona was trying to reach an agreement with the 7,700 persons holding contracts for homesites that could not be delivered. The company offered a series of options: the contract holders could have their principal and interest payments refunded to them over a three-year period; they could simply hold onto their property and make no more payments until the court cases were decided; or they could transfer the principal and interest into another lot, home, or condo on Marco or any of the other eight locations in which Deltona had properties available. In these cases the land would be discounted to reflect prices at the time of the original purchase.

Because Deltona felt that most of the contract holders would agree to the transfer arrangement, the company guessed that $14.7 million would handle the cash refunds. So it established a trust for this amount. Into the trust it deposited deeds representing property it intended to sell. Neil Bahr's Land and Investment subsidiary was given the task of disposing of this property.

Deltona underestimated the flood of refund requests. Big Key, Barfield Bay, and the Collier-Read properties had been highly appealing with their plans for finger canals with access to rivers and the Gulf. The purchasers were mainly water lovers who had no interest in Deltona's other predominantly land-locked properties. Even Marco's interior did not interest them. Many, too, had lost faith in Deltona and wanted to dissociate themselves from the company. Thus a year later Deltona was forced to add $5.7 million more property parcels to the trust. Then in 1979, the company had to take a deep breath and supplement the trust with $15.2 million additional properties. Ultimately up to two thirds of the contract holders demanded refunds!

Deltona Forced to Sell its Choicest Properties

Deltona found itself in urgent need of money not only to meet the refunds but even to pay its day-to-day operating expenses. Thus Bahr sent mailings to brokers around the state informing them that the company was ready to deal. Quickly throughout Florida real estate circles it became known that the harassed company was conducting a fire sale.

One of the first properties to be disposed of in order to obtain money for operating expenses was the Town Center Mall, which was sold in 1977, along with shopping centers in Spring Hill and the town of Deltona to a Canadian group. The sale brought almost $4 million, with Marco probably accounting for $1.5.

The beachfront was especially alluring to prospective buyers. "We never intended to sell any of it," Bahr lamented. "We had reserved it for ourselves." The beach, after all, had been the island's main attraction from the earliest days. It was to the beachfront that Deltona had looked to reap its

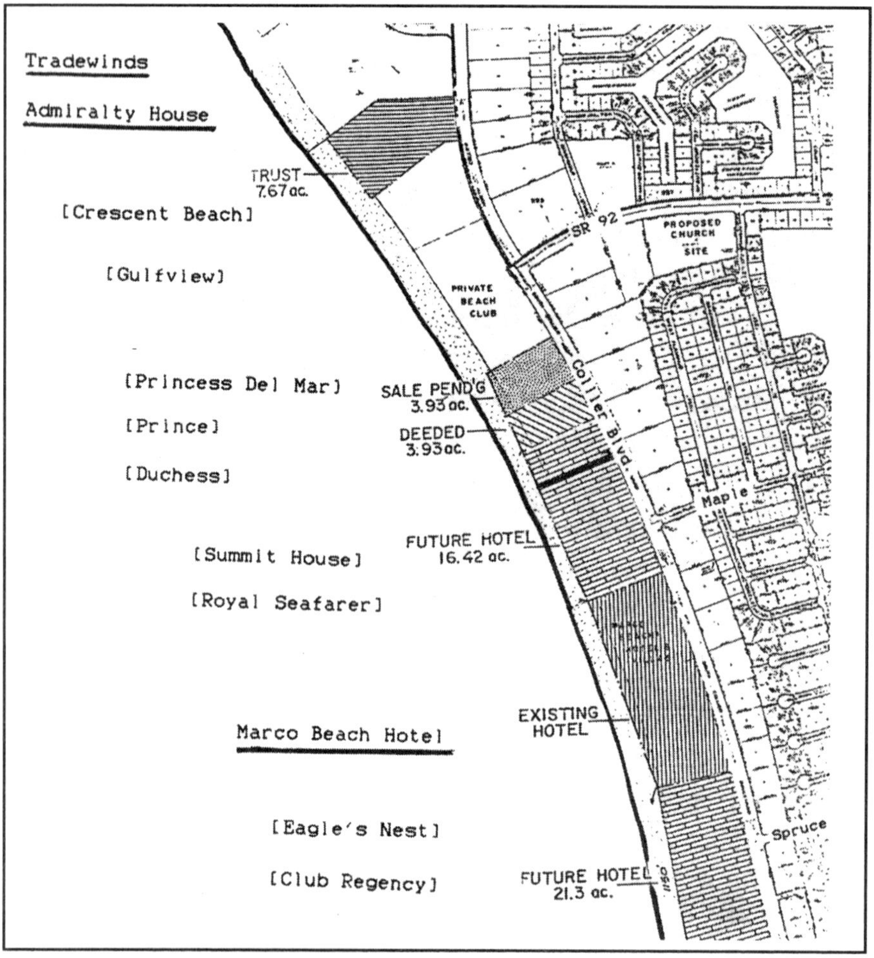

Crescent Beach in 1978, north segment.

This is an original Deltona sale status map showing the disposition of the valuable beachfront, which the company had been forced to put up for sale.

The lands marked "Trust" have been set aside to meet the anticipated refund demand due to the Corps' permit denial for Barfield Bay and Big Key. The other lots were being sold in order to meet bank interest and other operating expenses.

"Sale Pending" means negotiations were being conducted at the time this update was done. "Deeded" means the site has been sold.

The only buildings on this portion of the beach at this time were the Tradewinds, Admiralty House and Marco Beach Hotel, which would be sold to Marriott the following year. Future high rises have been added in brackets.

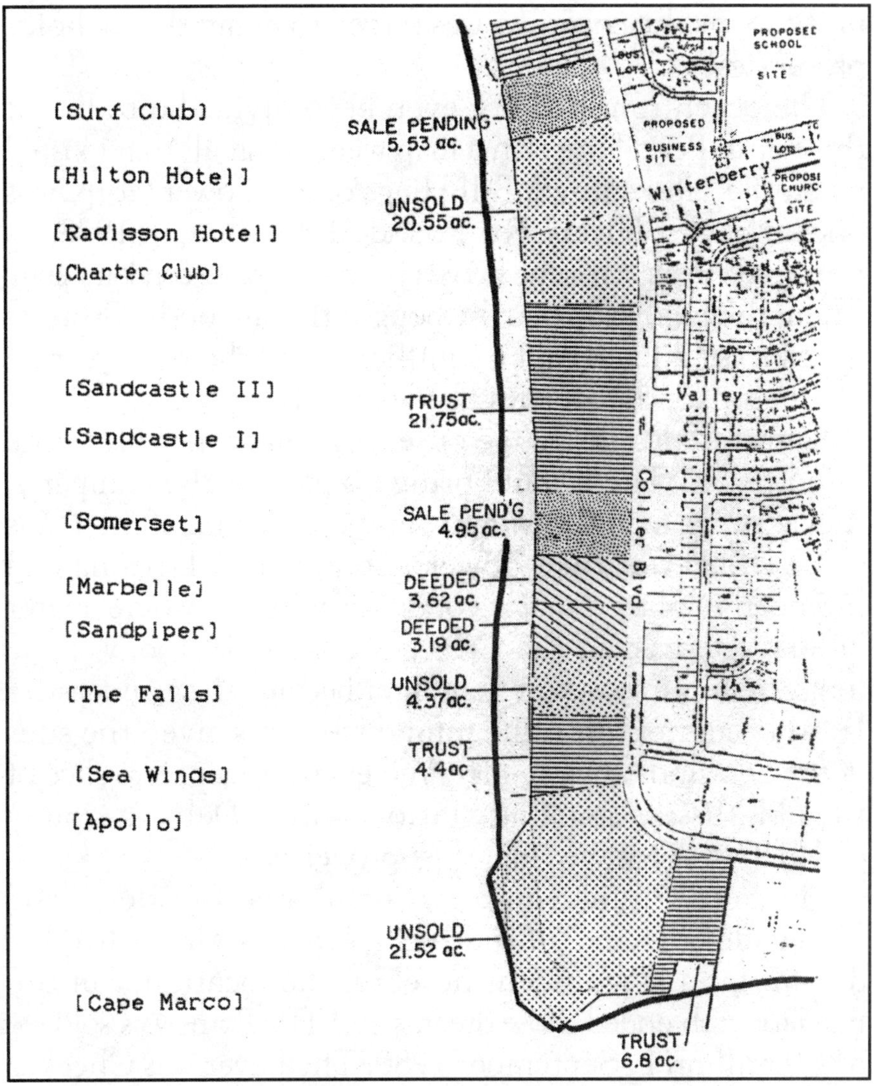

Crescent Beach in 1978, south segment.

Deltona sacrificed tremendous profits due to its forced sale of much of Crescent Beach. The company received around $350,000 per acre; but few years later the land had soared to $1 million an acre!

profit. Now the company was forced to dump those choice properties!

The beachfront had not even been divided into lots at this point. Pencil lines on a map were about all that existed when the sales started. Bill Higgs of the Power Corp. was one of the first buyers. For around $1.4 million in 1978, he purchased the site where he would put up the Prince condominium. Then, the following year, he bought the site of the Princess del Mar for a little over $1 million. And the next year he got the site of the Duchess for about $1.7 million.

Bahr was also in charge of selling the properties in the refund trust. They would bring no gain to the company; they were, in fact, throw-away properties. One of these was a site called the Twin Towers, upon which Deltona had intended to place a major condominium, but where a later builder constructed the Crescent Beach. So, too, was the long stretch of shoreline that later became the Sandcastles I and II. Father south the refund trust was given the sites of the Seawinds and Apollo. And even a seven-acre slice of the old Missile Tracking Station, which Deltona simply called The Point, became trust property.

The Point involved 30 acres and was considered the "creme de la creme" of the entire beach. Deltona had big dreams for a magnificent hotel on the location. But the need for cash ended those dreams and The Point was sold for $14.9 million in September 1980. The buyer was Checker Oil, said to be a subsidiary of Marathon Oil, and, through it, of U.S. Steel, whose own plans for development were likewise to be frustrated by business reversals.

The Sale of the Marco Beach Hotel, 1979

It was bad enough to have to sell The Point. But the real calamity was when the Marco Beach Hotel was put on the market. Nothing else had so epitomized the successes of Deltona. It was the jewel of the island. Yet it had to go. "That was the most bitter thing of all," Frank Mackle told me.

Many groups were interested in such a fine establishment, including the Hiltons. But Bahr decided on the Marriotts. The negotiations were lengthy and occasionally seemed to hinge on small items, such as assured starting times on the Marco Shores golf course, which Deltona had built three years earlier. Deltona asked $42 million even though it was carrying the hotel on its books for half that amount and its actual cost had been even lower. The price of $35 million was finally settled on, despite the Marriotts' complaint that they had not paid so much per room ever before. The Marriotts, in turn, immediately sold the hotel to the Massachusetts Mutual Life Insurance Co. for an undisclosed amount and a 25-year lease with options to renew for another 50 years.

Wild Speculation on the Beachfront

Many purchasers of the beachfront properties were speculators who intended to hold their lots only until prices peaked. Most were fantastically successful. Thus, whereas Deltona was forced to sell off Gulf parcels for around $350,000 per acre in 1978, a few years later the lot which would contain the Crescent Beach high rise was sold by an investor for $780,000 per acre.

Sometimes fortunes were made with surprising ease. Leonard Llewellyn told me how his three-man investment group bought the 14-acre parcel that would become the site of the Sandcastles I and II, the Charter Club, and the Radisson Hotel, held it for six months, and sold it for a profit of over $1.5 million!

Prices continued shooting upward. English tycoon, Alfred McAlpine, paid $1 million an acre when he bought the site of the Charter Club in 1980. The Hilton people shelled out $8.5 million to speculators for their hotel site in an area where Deltona had reluctantly disposed of similar lots for a third of that.

By 1988, the Gulf-front bristled with so many high rises that the county assessor valued them at 40 percent of the entire island! Because of the permit denials Deltona had given away a fortune!

The Hideaway Beach Story

The far northern part of the shoreline did not participate in the rocketing prices. This was the area that Deltona called Royal Marco Point. It was a long thumb of land upon which Deltona owned 90 acres at the tip and Jake Rupert owned the lower 211 acres. Rupert, head of a beer company bearing his name as well as of Yankee Stadium in New York, had been a friend of Barron Collier and had purchased his part of the peninsula at around the time Collier was buying up the rest of the island.

When Deltona took over from the Colliers, it planned to build a marina along with 100 homesites on its segment. The company approached Rupert to sell his portion but the offer was rejected, for there were bitter feelings between Rupert and Deltona, due at least partially to the fact that Rupert had to provide Deltona access to its property through his holdings.

Rumor has it that the Rupert family vowed never to sell to Deltona. In 1978 Rupert's estate sold out to a Canadian. Thus Deltona was unable to round out control of the peninsula and two years later the company disposed of its holdings to the Canadian for $5.2 million, or a mere $58,000 per acre.

Frank Mackle Park

Deltona was trimming its sails in other areas of Marco, too. In 1976 Frank Mackle announced that he had given up plans to build an executive golf course and tennis courts in a 60-acre area between South Heathwood Drive and Sandhill Street. The Griffis-Vogstad parcel, which Deltona had purchased from two daughters of Tommie Barfield some three years earlier, was not suitable for waterways. For this reason, as well as a general public-spiritedness, Mackle donated nine acres to the Marco Island Youth Center. It was named in his honor.

The Fabulous South Seas Project

Deltona was struggling but was not dead. Frank Mackle was now sole head of the company, for Robert had resigned early in 1977. Frank had always been the unquestioned leader and now, as board chairman and with his son, Frank III, beside him as president, Deltona set out on a course that, in retrospect, can only cause an observer to gasp at its daring.

Although Deltona had sold most of its vaunted beachfront, it had not disposed of three major segments. Highly desirable was a large, 55-acre piece of land extending back to Clam Bay. Development of this land had been sidetracked by the Corps' 1971 decree stopping all work in the Collier Bay permit area. Now, with Collier Bay approved, development could begin.

The South Seas Club was the most ambitious project on which Deltona would ever embark. It would take four years to complete and would consist of four huge condominium towers facing the Gulf along with 32 other buildings ranging from 7- story structures to some of just two

South Seas Club, 1978.

Deltona's Annual Report of 1978 had this full-page photo of the South Seas Club in its early stages.

Clam Bay is on the left. Lining the Gulf are the company's earliest condos: the Sunset Houses North and South, the Emerald Beach, the Tradewinds (at an angle), and the Admiralty House. The tall rectangular building farther on is the Gulf View. In the distance lies the Marco Beach Hotel to be sold to the Marriott chain the following year.

Across Caxambas Pass in the far distance is the long outline of Kice Island, once on Deltona's list of developments.

floors. There were 10 tennis courts, 172 boat slips on Clam Bay, and a liberal scattering of swimming pools.

It was dazzling both in its conception and its execution. Deltona took great pride in the fact that, despite its size, the South Seas Club was completed right on schedule and all units were delivered to purchasers exactly when promised. It showed what the company could do when it was not shackled by government regulations.

Deltona proudly featured its South Seas Club in its 1980 and 1981 annual reports.

The Ultimate in Luxury: The Summit House

Meanwhile, farther south on the beach, Deltona went on another ambitious building spree. Although the site had originally been designated for a moderate-priced hotel, Deltona needed quick profits, so it decided to construct the island's most luxurious condo. Thus the Summit House rose in twenty-two stories of unparalleled elegance. Its amenities were such that Frank Mackle himself would occupy a suite there. So great was the demand for units that the Summit House was virtually sold out even before it was completed in 1982!

At the same time the sleek tower of the Royal Seafarer rose beside the Summit House – both condominiums containing 128 units. It was released for sale two years before it was completed and sold-out in six months!

The Surf Club: An Experiment in Time-sharing

Down the Gulf-front from the Marco Beach Hotel, Deltona put up the Surf Club. The purpose of the Surf Club was to take advantage of the new time-sharing concept that was sweeping the nation. The Eagle's Nest time-share, which had been completed in 1980 was not built by Deltona, but it had been an instant success and may have provided the inspiration for Deltona's foray into this area.

The idea was that many persons wanted to enjoy Marco for only a few weeks out of the year. These persons did not want the expense of owning a year-round condo. Thus for an investment of between $6, 100 to $15,200, depending on the week and the location, one could have an apartment at the Surf Club with a view and amenities that matched those of year-round condos costing 10 times that amount. Deltona felt that the Surf Club could capture an important segment of this market.

The Surf Club was designed with a pair of handsome pink wings. The south wing was completed in 1983. The north was put off until the viability of the time-share concept was established.

The Completion of the Collier Bay/ Smokehouse Bay Area

Although the beachfront was Deltona's main center of activity during the late 1970 and early 1980s, the company wanted to finish off the Collier Bay permit area. No sooner had the Corps given approval, than Deltona dispatched an army of earth-moving equipment into the area to resume work on 1,400 homesites. The company had been stopped so abruptly in 1971 by Corps decree that large piles of dirt

The central commercial district 1980.

We are looking northeast with Collier Boulevard crossing the photo from top to bottom and Bald Eagle (S.R. 953) from left to right.

The large bare area in the foreground has just been raised by dredgings from Smokehouse Bay. This had been made possible by approval of the dredge and fill permit by the Army Corps of Engineers in 1976. Elkcam Circle forms the photo's lower perimeter.

Work is just beginning on the Royal Palm Mall. Onto this site 90 such businesses as McDonalds and the Barnett Bank were planned.

The Town Center Mall is across Bald Eagle and the Island Plaza Shopping Center across Collier Boulevard. The SunBank Centre will be constructed on the still-vacant northeast corner in the late 1980s.

had not been leveled and 40 homes had been left partially built.

Now work went on day and night. Within the year Hyacinth, Giralda, and Embassy courts were formed in Collier Bay. And where Collier merged with Smokehouse Bay the long fingers of Nautilus, Plantation, and Tigertail courts protruded into what had originally been a narrow, sluggish channel between the two bodies of water. Within Smokehouse Bay, Crescent Street was constructed along with its offshoots: Solana, Thrush, and Cameo courts.

Meanwhile, deep within what remained of the old Unit Six swamp, Goldenrod Avenue was at last constructed west from Bald Eagle all the way to the old air strip, which became Edgewater Court. Air traffic was moved to the new landing field which was completed on Marco Shores at the end of 1976.

Work is Resumed on the Central Business District

Deltona also resumed creating the business area on the west side of the Bald Eagle Drive and Collier Boulevard junction. Massive amounts of material were sucked up from Smokehouse Bay deepening it while, at the same time, filling the marsh that had served as the town dump.

Under ordinary circumstances Deltona would have built shopping centers on each of the corners and run them for profit the way it had the Town Center Mall. But the refunds due for Barfield and Big Key had changed the company's commercial operations completely. Pressed for quick cash, Deltona had to sell the land to other developers, who put up the Island Plaza on the northwest corner and, in 1982, the Royal Palm Mall on the southwest corner.

The Birth of Tigertail Beach

The Corps shutdown of 1971 had included work on the beach that Deltona had given the county two years earlier and which had been named after Tigertail Avenue, the main access road. (Tigertail Avenue had been so named because of its curling shape.)

The sudden halt of work had left a large pile of dirt on Blackmore Street near the planned entry to Tigertail Beach.

The Tigertail Beach area, 1970.

The beach will not be developed for another six years, due to the Army Corps' cease and desist order issued in 1971 and not rescinded until the Collier Bay permit was issued in 1976. Then a bridge will be constructed at the end of Hernando Drive and a parking lot installed.

At the time this photo was taken the landfill that will become Blackmore, Henderson, and Cottage Courts has just emerged from the swamps around the outlet of Clam Bay beyond the photo to the left. The gigantic South Seas complex will be built in the early 1980s on the far side of the outlet.

Kendall Drive, entry to Hideaway Beach, is mostly just part of the ditch used to form a mosquito dike around the Blackmore Court group.

Now this accumulation was removed and a bridge constructed over the Clam Bay outlet. Thus, finally, public access could be gained to Crescent Beach.

Development of Marco Shores Begins

Although the excitement centered along the Gulf, Deltona also reached into the mainland portion of its Marco holdings. Having already developed a fine golf course at

Marco Shores in the early 1980s.

Deltona's long-range plans envisioned the development of the entire area encompassed in this photo.

The airport, which opened in 1976, is in the foreground, The Tropic Schooner apartments nestle between a small lake and the golf course. McIlvane Bay is the long body of water bordering Marco Shores on the left. The S.R. 951 causeway crosses McIlvane in the distance. Mainsail Drive runs from the airport to S.R. 951. In the distance at the extreme left rise two of Deltona's South Sea Club towers on Marco Island. In the middle distance lies the Isles of Capri development. To its right is the Collier-Read Tract. Deltona designated Collier-Read as a major development similar to Marco Island. Rookery Bay, the Conservancy's nature preserve, lies at the extreme upper right.

Marco Shores, Deltona constructed a huge complex called the Tropic Schooner in 1982. Containing 239 units, it was almost as large as the Summit House and the Royal Seafarer together. It consisted of two-story, "garden-style" buildings with the emphasis on golf and tennis rather than the beach and boating. Deltona intended to expand the community to 1,500 buildings in the immediate future.

The Money for Construction

How was it that a company so close to bankruptcy could indulge in such a frenzy of construction? From where were the funds coming?

The answer is that bankers almost lined up to make loans to Deltona. There were two reasons for this. The first involved the esteem with which Frank Mackle was held by the banking community. The second revolved around the conviction in financial circles that Deltona had been wrongly treated by the Army Corps and that, as a result of the favorable ruling by the District Court of Claims in 1980, either the permit ban would soon be rescinded or Deltona would be awarded a large compensation for its loss of buildable land. Furthermore, the demand for Marco properties was extremely high and Deltona was poised to take advantage of this demand.

The sums made available were staggering. In 1976 Deltona received just $4 million in construction loans. By 1980, when its building orgy began in earnest, it received $63 million! The next year it bargained for $96 million more – and the year following almost that much again! Within the short period between 1980 and 1984 Deltona received a third of a billion dollars from the banks!

These sums enabled Deltona to engage in its almost incredible building adventure. When it was over, seven major high rises had been constructed along with almost innumerable low-rise buildings.

But there were a pair of vital questions upon which it all hinged: would sales in these new units be sufficient to pay the almost astronomical interest the construction loans required?; and would Deltona's suit against the Army Corps, under appeal for two years, secure it the additional funds it so desperately needed?

The lawsuit question was answered first.

10

The Dream Ends, 1984-86

Deltona had been encouraged by the 1980 Court of Claims ruling that either the Corps must lift its dredging denial or the company must receive compensation for the lands for which the dredge and fill permit had been denied. Although compensation had not been set, Deltona believed that the permit denials cost it at least $100 million!

But the ruling had been appealed and all parties were waiting for the new decision.

The Final Court Decisions

Deltona also had another lawsuit pending. This suit questioned the very constitutionality of the Corps' action. Deltona placed great faith in this assertion. But in January 1981, the District Court found that the Corps acted within the Constitution.

Eight months later the Court of Claims reached a decision on the compensation case. Deltona had pinned a good many of its hopes on winning this case for a second, and last time. But the finding here, too, was against the company. Deltona then petitioned the U.S. Supreme Court to review this decision. On March 22, 1982 the Supreme Court refused this request.

Surrender to the Environmentalists, 1982

Deltona had reached the end of its course of legal action. Accordingly, four months later it signed to a surrender document with various state regulatory agencies and the Conservancy, the Audubon Society, and other environmentalist groups. In it Deltona agreed to turn nearly all its undeveloped holdings on Marco Island and Marco Shores into nature preserves. The Collier-Read Tract, which Deltona had planned for homesites as lovely as those on Marco Island, was deeded outright to the state of Florida for inclusion in the Rookery Bay Sanctuary.

In return the company was permitted to put 300 units on Horr's Island uplands and up to 600 single family and 10,000 multifamily units at Marco Shores. But this was never done, for none of these developments would have the finger canals that made Marco Island so desirable. Marco Shores, being inland, would be just another struggling development in south Florida, which was not the most appealing place during the summer heat.

Problems at Marco Shores and at the Surf Club

The monstrous load of bank loans demanded substantial sales to meet the payments. But they were not coming with the anticipated numbers.

Marco Shores was one problem. Even though Deltona ballyhooed the development during 1983 and 1984, it was not a viable community at this time. Although it had an airport and a fine golf course, the first attempt at large-scale colonization in the form of the Tropic Schooner was not a success. Prospective residents wanted to reside on Marco Island, with its wending canals and marvelous beach. They found no allure in the hot inlands, despite its golfing greenery. Frank Mackle even called back temporarily his ace sales director, Neil Bahr. But to little avail.

Another problem developed with the Surf Club. Deltona had seriously miscalculated the appeal of time-sharing. Although the choice winter weeks were snapped up, sales of less desirable weeks went very slowly. Construction of the Surf Club's second, northern, wing was postponed.

Deltona was not alone in having problems with its time-share condo. For many years time-sharing was a bane on the entire central portion of Crescent Beach. A Canadian group built the Gulfside Club time-share just down from the Surf. The Gulfside was never a success and stood vacant for several years. It did not prosper until it was sold in 1986 and became the Radisson Hotel.

Next to the Radisson was the Charter Club, a pair of towers built in 1982 and 1983. Owned by the Alfred McAlpine Co., a major British corporation, the Charter Club could weather the slow times. But it took a decade for it to be more than 50 percent sold.

The South Seas Club: When a Sale is Not a Sale

The South Seas Club had been viewed as Deltona's salvation. The company felt certain that the complex, with its quartet of huge high-rise towers and myriad of low-rise resorts, tennis courts, swimming pools, and mooring docks, was sure to attract buyers.

In this Deltona was not mistaken. Sales were brisk. Yet a certain portion of these sales was actually in the form of transfers from Big Key, Barfield Bay, and the Collier-Read tract. The same held true for the other new buildings: the Summit House and the Royal Seafarer. Thus, when the totals were tallied during the big sale years of 1980 and 1981, the profits were far lower than expected.

In 1982, with a major recession, sales plunged. Deltona could not get rid of 1,200 condominium units and posted a $19 million loss. The next year there was another loss. And by 1984 the red ink had run up to $55 million over three years.

Deltona was in very bad straits. All its major assets not vital for day-to-day operations had been sold. Even the Marco Island golf and country club had been refinanced. Personnel had been cut from a high of over 4,000 in the 1970s, to just 745 rattling around the now-cavernous headquarters in Miami. Just to enable Deltona to continue operating, Frank Mackle, through the Mackle Co., loaned it $5 million. Even so, the company was no longer able to make payments on its bank loans.

Frank Mackle Resigns

By 1985 Frank Mackle could see that the end was approaching. He was now 67 years old and, though the fires still burned, time was no longer on his side. Deltona, as it had become, was just a shell of his dreams. Both his brothers had left the company and both were dead. Bahr, his trusted friend, often called the fourth Mackle brother, was occupied in the separate Deltona subsidiary selling off assets. Vensel who had been with Mackle from the first, had planned Marco and had been the key official dealing with the Corps and the environmentalists had left to start his own architectural firm. Even Herb Savage, designer of the impressive Marco Beach Hotel, as well as many other company landmarks, was off on his own.

Other companies began to view Deltona as prey. Empire of Carolina, a toy manufacturer, was one. Early in 1986 it began a hostile stock buy-out designed to force Frank Mackle and his son, Frank III, from leadership of Deltona. Because the Mackle family owned or controlled only about 15 percent of Deltona's common stock, Frank Mackle turned to the Topeka Group, part of Minnesota Power, to save the company. Ironically, Topeka's interest in Deltona centered more on its utilities than its development business. Topeka came to Deltona's rescue and thereby the utilities fell under control of Topeka's subsidiary, Southern States Utilities.

With Deltona now in friendly hands, on March 4, 1986 Frank and his son submitted their resignations. The dream was over.

Epilogue – 1986

It is over a decade since Frank Mackle resigned from Deltona. Sometimes he stands before the great glass windows in his suite at the Summit House and looks at the wonders he has wrought. Once in a while he recalls the first day he was on Marco, when he stood on the shore with his brothers and saw only scrubby dunes and Crescent Beach, lonely and deserted, glistening in the sun.

Such dreams there were that day. And many of them came true.

All could have come true but for the denial of the two vital dredge and fill permits. Even now it hurts. "The Corps didn't play fair with us," he told me. Yet, oddly, these very denials, with the precedent they set, made Marco Island unique. Never again would such a waterfront development of finger canals be allowed. Marco became, in effect, America's last such paradise.

Mackle's long years with Deltona ended unceremoniously. "There was no fanfare when I left headquarters for the last time," he recalled. "I got no gold watch. I simply wished the new owners luck and walked out."

But resigning did not erase his memories of what was and what might have been. Although these memories are not as vivid as they once were, they remain. "It's like General MacArthur put it," Mackle mused, "old soldiers never die, they just fade away."

BIBLIOGRAPHY

Allan, Leslie, Beryl Kuder and Sarah Oakes. *Promised Lands*. New York: Inform Inc., 1977.

Bahr, Neil. Interviews with author. 1990-1992.

Carter, Luther J. *The Florida Experience: Land and Water Policy in a Growth State*. Baltimore, M.D.: John Hopkins University Press. 1974.

————————."Denial of Marco Permits." *Science*, May 1976.

Conservancy, Yearbook. 1990.

DeGeorge, Gail. "Florida's Land Giant Eyes a Prize." *Business Week*, May 16, 1988.

Deltona. *Annual Reports*. 1962-1991.

Deltona's letters and newspaper clippings relating to the dredge and fill permit proceedings, 1963-83. (More than 400 documents).

"Deltona Out of the Swamp." *Forbes*, March 16, 1981.

Downey, Wesley. Interview with author. 1991.

"Earthmoving magic." *Professional Builder*, April 1970.

Hancock, A. C. Interview with author. 1991.

Herren, Norman. Interview with author. 1991.

Hinkley, C. Edward. Interview with author. 1991.

Llewellyn, Leonard. Interviews with author. 1990-92.

Mackle, Frank Jr. Interviews with author. 1990-92.

Marco Island Chamber of Commerce publications.

Marco Island Eagle. Issues from 1970-92.

Minch, Barbara. Interviews with author. 1990-92.

Miami Herald. January 3, 1965 and January 2, 1972.

Moser, Don. "Mangrove Island is Reprieved by Army Engineers." *Smithsonian*, January 1977.

Naples Daily News. September 2-3, 1975. Also other issues 1975-92.

Orlando Evening Star. December 17-26, 1968 (for the Barbara Mackle story).

Savage, Herbert. Interviews with author. 1991-92.

Seneker, Harold. "Deltona in Deep Trouble." *Forbes*, October 1, 1976.

Settlement Agreement of 1982.

Tebeau, Charlton W. *Florida's Last Frontier*, Miami: University of Miami Press, 1966.

U. S. District Court, "Deltona Corp. v. Alexander", Secretary of the Army. January 14, 1981.

U. S. Court of Claims, "Deltona Corp. v. The United States". August 19, 1981.

Vensel, James. Interviews with author. 1990-92.

Yokel, Bernard. Interviews with author. 1991.

Index